Life Application Bible Studies
2 CORINTHIANS

APPLICATION® BIBLE STUDIES

Part 1:
Complete text of 2 Corinthians with study notes and features from the *Life Application Study Bible*

Part 2:
Thirteen lessons for individual or group study

Study questions written and edited by

Rev. Michael R. Marcey
Rev. David R. Veerman
Dr. James C. Galvin
Dr. Bruce B. Barton

New Living Translation®

Tyndale House Publishers, Inc.
Carol Stream, Illinois

2 corinthians

CONTENTS

A NOTE TO READERS

The *Holy Bible,* New Living Translation, was first published in 1996. It quickly became one of the most popular Bible translations in the English-speaking world. While the NLT's influence was rapidly growing, the Bible Translation Committee determined that an additional investment in scholarly review and text refinement could make it even better. So shortly after its initial publication, the committee began an eight-year process with the purpose of increasing the level of the NLT's precision without sacrificing its easy-to-understand quality. This second-generation text was completed in 2004 and is reflected in this edition of the New Living Translation. An additional update with minor changes was subsequently introduced in 2007.

The goal of any Bible translation is to convey the meaning and content of the ancient Hebrew, Aramaic, and Greek texts as accurately as possible to contemporary readers. The challenge for our translators was to create a text that would communicate as clearly and powerfully to today's readers as the original texts did to readers and listeners in the ancient biblical world. The resulting translation is easy to read and understand, while also accurately communicating the meaning and content of the original biblical texts. The NLT is a general-purpose text especially good for study, devotional reading, and reading aloud in worship services.

We believe that the New Living Translation—which combines the latest biblical scholarship with a clear, dynamic writing style—will communicate God's word powerfully to all who read it. We publish it with the prayer that God will use it to speak his timeless truth to the church and the world in a fresh, new way.

The Publishers
October 2007

INTRODUCTION TO THE
NEW LIVING TRANSLATION

Translation Philosophy and Methodology

English Bible translations tend to be governed by one of two general translation theories. The first theory has been called "formal-equivalence," "literal," or "word-for-word" translation. According to this theory, the translator attempts to render each word of the original language into English and seeks to preserve the original syntax and sentence structure as much as possible in translation. The second theory has been called "dynamic-equivalence," "functional-equivalence," or "thought-for-thought" translation. The goal of this translation theory is to produce in English the closest natural equivalent of the message expressed by the original-language text, both in meaning and in style.

Both of these translation theories have their strengths. A formal-equivalence translation preserves aspects of the original text—including ancient idioms, term consistency, and original-language syntax—that are valuable for scholars and professional study. It allows a reader to trace formal elements of the original-language text through the English translation. A dynamic-equivalence translation, on the other hand, focuses on translating the message of the original-language text. It ensures that the meaning of the text is readily apparent to the contemporary reader. This allows the message to come through with immediacy, without requiring the reader to struggle with foreign idioms and awkward syntax. It also facilitates serious study of the text's message and clarity in both devotional and public reading.

The pure application of either of these translation philosophies would create translations at opposite ends of the translation spectrum. But in reality, all translations contain a mixture of these two philosophies. A purely formal-equivalence translation would be unintelligible in English, and a purely dynamic-equivalence translation would risk being unfaithful to the original. That is why translations shaped by dynamic-equivalence theory are usually quite literal when the original text is relatively clear, and the translations shaped by formal-equivalence theory are sometimes quite dynamic when the original text is obscure.

The translators of the New Living Translation set out to render the message of the original texts of Scripture into clear, contemporary English. As they did so, they kept the concerns of both formal-equivalence and dynamic-equivalence in mind. On the one hand, they translated as simply and literally as possible when that approach yielded an accurate, clear, and natural English text. Many words and phrases were rendered literally and consistently into English, preserving essential literary and rhetorical devices, ancient metaphors, and word choices that give structure to the text and provide echoes of meaning from one passage to the next.

On the other hand, the translators rendered the message more dynamically when the literal rendering was hard to understand, was misleading, or yielded archaic or foreign wording. They clarified difficult metaphors and terms to aid in the reader's understanding. The translators first struggled with the meaning of the words and phrases in the ancient context; then they rendered the message into clear, natural English. Their goal was to be both faithful to the ancient texts and eminently readable. The result is a translation that is both exegetically accurate and idiomatically powerful.

Translation Process and Team

To produce an accurate translation of the Bible into contemporary English, the translation team needed the skills necessary to enter into the thought patterns of the ancient authors and then to render their ideas, connotations, and effects into clear, contemporary English.

To begin this process, qualified biblical scholars were needed to interpret the meaning of the original text and to check it against our base English translation. In order to guard against personal and theological biases, the scholars needed to represent a diverse group of evangelicals who would employ the best exegetical tools. Then to work alongside the scholars, skilled English stylists were needed to shape the text into clear, contemporary English.

With these concerns in mind, the Bible Translation Committee recruited teams of scholars that represented a broad spectrum of denominations, theological perspectives, and backgrounds within the worldwide evangelical community. Each book of the Bible was assigned to three different scholars with proven expertise in the book or group of books to be reviewed. Each of these scholars made a thorough review of a base translation and submitted suggested revisions to the appropriate Senior Translator. The Senior Translator then reviewed and summarized these suggestions and proposed a first-draft revision of the base text. This draft served as the basis for several additional phases of exegetical and stylistic committee review. Then the Bible Translation Committee jointly reviewed and approved every verse of the final translation.

Throughout the translation and editing process, the Senior Translators and their scholar teams were given a chance to review the editing done by the team of stylists. This ensured that exegetical errors would not be introduced late in the process and that the entire Bible Translation Committee was happy with the final result. By choosing a team of qualified scholars and skilled stylists and by setting up a process that allowed their interaction throughout the process, the New Living Translation has been refined to preserve the essential formal elements of the original biblical texts, while also creating a clear, understandable English text.

The New Living Translation was first published in 1996. Shortly after its initial publication, the Bible Translation Committee began a process of further committee review and translation refinement. The purpose of this continued revision was to increase the level of precision without sacrificing the text's easy-to-understand quality. This second-edition text was completed in 2004, and an additional update with minor changes was subsequently introduced in 2007. This printing of the New Living Translation reflects the updated 2007 text.

Written to Be Read Aloud
It is evident in Scripture that the biblical documents were written to be read aloud, often in public worship (see Nehemiah 8; Luke 4:16-20; 1 Timothy 4:13; Revelation 1:3). It is still the case today that more people will hear the Bible read aloud in church than are likely to read it for themselves. Therefore, a new translation must communicate with clarity and power when it is read publicly. Clarity was a primary goal for the NLT translators, not only to facilitate private reading and understanding, but also to ensure that it would be excellent for public reading and make an immediate and powerful impact on any listener.

The Texts behind the New Living Translation
The Old Testament translators used the Masoretic Text of the Hebrew Bible as represented in *Biblia Hebraica Stuttgartensia* (1977), with its extensive system of textual notes; this is an update of Rudolf Kittel's *Biblia Hebraica* (Stuttgart, 1937). The translators also further compared the Dead Sea Scrolls, the Septuagint and other Greek manuscripts, the Samaritan Pentateuch, the Syriac Peshitta, the Latin Vulgate, and any other versions or manuscripts that shed light on the meaning of difficult passages.

The New Testament translators used the two standard editions of the Greek New Testament: the *Greek New Testament*, published by the United Bible Societies (UBS, fourth revised edition, 1993), and *Novum Testamentum Graece*, edited by Nestle and Aland (NA, twenty-seventh edition, 1993). These two editions, which have the same text but differ in punctuation and textual notes, represent, for the most part, the best in modern textual scholarship. However, in cases where strong textual or other scholarly evidence supported the decision, the translators sometimes chose to differ from the UBS and NA Greek texts and followed variant readings found in other ancient witnesses. Significant textual variants of this sort are always noted in the textual notes of the New Living Translation.

Translation Issues
The translators have made a conscious effort to provide a text that can be easily understood by the typical reader of modern English. To this end, we sought to use only vocabulary and

language structures in common use today. We avoided using language likely to become quickly dated or that reflects only a narrow subdialect of English, with the goal of making the New Living Translation as broadly useful and timeless as possible.

But our concern for readability goes beyond the concerns of vocabulary and sentence structure. We are also concerned about historical and cultural barriers to understanding the Bible, and we have sought to translate terms shrouded in history and culture in ways that can be immediately understood. To this end:

- We have converted ancient weights and measures (for example, "ephah" [a unit of dry volume] or "cubit" [a unit of length]) to modern English (American) equivalents, since the ancient measures are not generally meaningful to today's readers. Then in the textual footnotes we offer the literal Hebrew, Aramaic, or Greek measures, along with modern metric equivalents.

- Instead of translating ancient currency values literally, we have expressed them in common terms that communicate the message. For example, in the Old Testament, "ten shekels of silver" becomes "ten pieces of silver" to convey the intended message. In the New Testament, we have often translated the "denarius" as "the normal daily wage" to facilitate understanding. Then a footnote offers: "Greek *a denarius,* the payment for a full day's wage." In general, we give a clear English rendering and then state the literal Hebrew, Aramaic, or Greek in a textual footnote.

- Since the names of Hebrew months are unknown to most contemporary readers, and since the Hebrew lunar calendar fluctuates from year to year in relation to the solar calendar used today, we have looked for clear ways to communicate the time of year the Hebrew months (such as Abib) refer to. When an expanded or interpretive rendering is given in the text, a textual note gives the literal rendering. Where it is possible to define a specific ancient date in terms of our modern calendar, we use modern dates in the text. A textual footnote then gives the literal Hebrew date and states the rationale for our rendering. For example, Ezra 6:15 pinpoints the date when the postexilic Temple was completed in Jerusalem: "the third day of the month Adar." This was during the sixth year of King Darius's reign (that is, 515 B.C.). We have translated that date as March 12, with a footnote giving the Hebrew and identifying the year as 515 B.C.

- Since ancient references to the time of day differ from our modern methods of denoting time, we have used renderings that are instantly understandable to the modern reader. Accordingly, we have rendered specific times of day by using approximate equivalents in terms of our common "o'clock" system. On occasion, translations such as "at dawn the next morning" or "as the sun was setting" have been used when the biblical reference is more general.

- When the meaning of a proper name (or a wordplay inherent in a proper name) is relevant to the message of the text, its meaning is often illuminated with a textual footnote. For example, in Exodus 2:10 the text reads: "The princess named him Moses, for she explained, 'I lifted him out of the water.' " The accompanying footnote reads: "*Moses* sounds like a Hebrew term that means 'to lift out.' "

    Sometimes, when the actual meaning of a name is clear, that meaning is included in parentheses within the text itself. For example, the text at Genesis 16:11 reads: "You are to name him Ishmael *(which means 'God hears'),* for the LORD has heard your cry of distress." Since the original hearers and readers would have instantly understood the meaning of the name "Ishmael," we have provided modern readers with the same information so they can experience the text in a similar way.

- Many words and phrases carry a great deal of cultural meaning that was obvious to the original readers but needs explanation in our own culture. For example, the phrase "they beat their breasts" (Luke 23:48) in ancient times meant that people were very upset, often in mourning. In our translation we chose to translate this phrase dynamically for clarity: "They went home *in deep sorrow.*" Then we included a footnote with the literal Greek, which reads: "Greek *went home beating their breasts.*" In other similar cases, however, we have sometimes chosen to illuminate the existing literal expression to make it immediately understandable. For example, here we might have expanded the literal Greek phrase to read: "They went home beating their breasts *in sorrow.*" If we had done this, we would not have included a textual footnote, since the literal Greek clearly appears in translation.

- Metaphorical language is sometimes difficult for contemporary readers to understand, so at times we have chosen to translate or illuminate the meaning of a metaphor. For example, the ancient poet writes, "Your neck is *like* the tower of David" (Song of Songs 4:4). We have rendered it "Your neck is *as beautiful as* the tower of David" to clarify the intended positive meaning of the simile. Another example comes in Ecclesiastes 12:3, which can be literally rendered: "Remember him . . . when the grinding women cease because they are few, and the women who look through the windows see dimly." We have rendered it: "Remember him before your teeth—your few remaining servants—stop grinding; and before your eyes—the women looking through the windows—see dimly." We clarified such metaphors only when we believed a typical reader might be confused by the literal text.

- When the content of the original language text is poetic in character, we have rendered it in English poetic form. We sought to break lines in ways that clarify and highlight the relationships between phrases of the text. Hebrew poetry often uses parallelism, a literary form where a second phrase (or in some instances a third or fourth) echoes the initial phrase in some way. In Hebrew parallelism, the subsequent parallel phrases continue, while also furthering and sharpening, the thought expressed in the initial line or phrase. Whenever possible, we sought to represent these parallel phrases in natural poetic English.

- The Greek term *hoi Ioudaioi* is literally translated "the Jews" in many English translations. In the Gospel of John, however, this term doesn't always refer to the Jewish people generally. In some contexts, it refers more particularly to the Jewish religious leaders. We have attempted to capture the meaning in these different contexts by using terms such as "the people" (with a footnote: Greek *the Jewish people*) or "the religious leaders," where appropriate.

- One challenge we faced was how to translate accurately the ancient biblical text that was originally written in a context where male-oriented terms were used to refer to humanity generally. We needed to respect the nature of the ancient context while also trying to make the translation clear to a modern audience that tends to read male-oriented language as applying only to males. Often the original text, though using masculine nouns and pronouns, clearly intends that the message be applied to both men and women. A typical example is found in the New Testament letters, where the believers are called "brothers" (*adelphoi*). Yet it is clear from the content of these letters that they were addressed to all the believers—male and female. Thus, we have usually translated this Greek word as "brothers and sisters" in order to represent the historical situation more accurately.

    We have also been sensitive to passages where the text applies generally to human beings or to the human condition. In some instances we have used plural pronouns (they, them) in place of the masculine singular (he, him). For example, a traditional rendering of Proverbs 22:6 is: "Train up a child in the way he should go, and when he is old he will not turn from it." We have rendered it: "Direct your children onto the right path, and when they are older, they will not leave it." At times, we have also replaced third person pronouns with the second person to ensure clarity. A traditional rendering of Proverbs 26:27 is: "He who digs a pit will fall into it, and he who rolls a stone, it will come back on him." We have rendered it: "If you set a trap for others, you will get caught in it yourself. If you roll a boulder down on others, it will crush you instead."

    We should emphasize, however, that all masculine nouns and pronouns used to represent God (for example, "Father") have been maintained without exception. All decisions of this kind have been driven by the concern to reflect accurately the intended meaning of the original texts of Scripture.

Lexical Consistency in Terminology

For the sake of clarity, we have translated certain original-language terms consistently, especially within synoptic passages and for commonly repeated rhetorical phrases, and within certain word categories such as divine names and non-theological technical terminology (e.g., liturgical, legal, cultural, zoological, and botanical terms). For theological terms, we have allowed a greater semantic range of acceptable English words or phrases for a single Hebrew or Greek word. We have avoided some theological terms that are not readily understood by many modern readers. For example, we avoided using words such as "justification" and "sanctification," which are carryovers from Latin translations. In place of these words, we have provided renderings such as "made right with God" and "made holy."

The Spelling of Proper Names

Many individuals in the Bible, especially the Old Testament, are known by more than one name (e.g., Uzziah/Azariah). For the sake of clarity, we have tried to use a single spelling for any one individual, footnoting the literal spelling whenever we differ from it. This is especially helpful in delineating the kings of Israel and Judah. King Joash/Jehoash of Israel has been consistently called Jehoash, while King Joash/Jehoash of Judah is called Joash. A similar distinction has been used to distinguish between Joram/Jehoram of Israel and Joram/Jehoram of Judah. All such decisions were made with the goal of clarifying the text for the reader. When the ancient biblical writers clearly had a theological purpose in their choice of a variant name (e.g., Esh-baal/Ishbosheth), the different names have been maintained with an explanatory footnote.

For the names Jacob and Israel, which are used interchangeably for both the individual patriarch and the nation, we generally render it "Israel" when it refers to the nation and "Jacob" when it refers to the individual. When our rendering of the name differs from the underlying Hebrew text, we provide a textual footnote, which includes this explanation: "The names 'Jacob' and 'Israel' are often interchanged throughout the Old Testament, referring sometimes to the individual patriarch and sometimes to the nation."

The Rendering of Divine Names

All appearances of *'el, 'elohim,* or *'eloah* have been translated "God," except where the context demands the translation "god(s)." We have generally rendered the tetragrammaton (*YHWH*) consistently as "the Lord," utilizing a form with small capitals that is common among English translations. This will distinguish it from the name *'adonai,* which we render "Lord." When *'adonai* and *YHWH* appear together, we have rendered it "Sovereign Lord." This also distinguishes *'adonai YHWH* from cases where *YHWH* appears with *'elohim,* which is rendered "Lord God." When *YH* (the short form of *YHWH*) and *YHWH* appear together, we have rendered it "Lord God." When *YHWH* appears with the term *tseba'oth,* we have rendered it "Lord of Heaven's Armies" to translate the meaning of the name. In a few cases, we have utilized the transliteration, *Yahweh,* when the personal character of the name is being invoked in contrast to another divine name or the name of some other god (for example, see Exodus 3:15; 6:2-3).

In the New Testament, the Greek word *christos* has been translated as "Messiah" when the context assumes a Jewish audience. When a Gentile audience can be assumed, *christos* has been translated as "Christ." The Greek word *kurios* is consistently translated "Lord," except that it is translated "Lord" wherever the New Testament text explicitly quotes from the Old Testament, and the text there has it in small capitals.

Textual Footnotes

The New Living Translation provides several kinds of textual footnotes, all designated in the text with an asterisk:

- When for the sake of clarity the NLT renders a difficult or potentially confusing phrase dynamically, we generally give the literal rendering in a textual footnote. This allows the reader to see the literal source of our dynamic rendering and how our translation relates to other more literal translations. These notes are prefaced with "Hebrew," "Aramaic," or "Greek," identifying the language of the underlying source text. For example, in Acts 2:42 we translated the literal "breaking of bread" (from the Greek) as "the Lord's Supper" to clarify that this verse refers to the ceremonial practice of the church rather than just an ordinary meal. Then we attached a footnote to "the Lord's Supper," which reads: "Greek *the breaking of bread.*"

- Textual footnotes are also used to show alternative renderings, prefaced with the word "Or." These normally occur for passages where an aspect of the meaning is debated. On occasion, we also provide notes on words or phrases that represent a departure from long-standing tradition. These notes are prefaced with "Tradition-ally rendered." For example, the footnote to the translation "serious skin disease" at Leviticus 13:2 says: "Traditionally rendered *leprosy*. The Hebrew word used throughout this passage is used to describe various skin diseases."

- When our translators follow a textual variant that differs significantly from our stan-dard Hebrew or Greek texts (listed earlier), we document that difference with a foot-note. We also footnote cases when the NLT excludes a passage that is included in the Greek text known as the *Textus Receptus* (and familiar to readers through its transla-tion in the King James Version). In such cases, we offer a translation of the excluded text in a footnote, even though it is generally recognized as a later addition to the Greek text and not part of the original Greek New Testament.

- All Old Testament passages that are quoted in the New Testament are identified by a textual footnote at the New Testament location. When the New Testament clearly quotes from the Greek translation of the Old Testament, and when it differs signifi-cantly in wording from the Hebrew text, we also place a textual footnote at the Old Testament location. This note includes a rendering of the Greek version, along with a cross-reference to the New Testament passage(s) where it is cited (for example, see notes on Psalms 8:2; 53:3; Proverbs 3:12).

- Some textual footnotes provide cultural and historical information on places, things, and people in the Bible that are probably obscure to modern readers. Such notes should aid the reader in understanding the message of the text. For example, in Acts 12:1, "King Herod" is named in this translation as "King Herod Agrippa" and is iden-tified in a footnote as being "the nephew of Herod Antipas and a grandson of Herod the Great."

- When the meaning of a proper name (or a wordplay inherent in a proper name) is relevant to the meaning of the text, it is either illuminated with a textual footnote or included within parentheses in the text itself. For example, the footnote concerning the name "Eve" at Genesis 3:20 reads: "*Eve* sounds like a Hebrew term that means 'to give life.'" This wordplay in the Hebrew illuminates the meaning of the text, which goes on to say that Eve "would be the mother of all who live."

As WE SUBMIT this translation for publication, we recognize that any translation of the Scrip-tures is subject to limitations and imperfections. Anyone who has attempted to communi-cate the richness of God's Word into another language will realize it is impossible to make a perfect translation. Recognizing these limitations, we sought God's guidance and wisdom throughout this project. Now we pray that he will accept our efforts and use this translation for the benefit of the church and of all people.

We pray that the New Living Translation will overcome some of the barriers of history, cul-ture, and language that have kept people from reading and understanding God's Word. We hope that readers unfamiliar with the Bible will find the words clear and easy to understand and that readers well versed in the Scriptures will gain a fresh perspective. We pray that readers will gain insight and wisdom for living, but most of all that they will meet the God of the Bible and be forever changed by knowing him.

The Bible Translation Committee
October 2007

WHY THE
LIFE APPLICATION STUDY BIBLE
IS UNIQUE

Have you ever opened your Bible and asked the following:

- What does this passage really mean?
- How does it apply to my life?
- Why does some of the Bible seem irrelevant?
- What do these ancient cultures have to do with today?
- I love God; why can't I understand what he is saying to me through his word?
- What's going on in the lives of these Bible people?

Many Christians do not read the Bible regularly. Why? Because in the pressures of daily living they cannot find a connection between the timeless principles of Scripture and the ever-present problems of day-by-day living.

God urges us to apply his word (Isaiah 42:23; 1 Corinthians 10:11; 2 Thessalonians 3:4), but too often we stop at accumulating Bible knowledge. This is why the *Life Application Study Bible* was developed—to show how to put into practice what we have learned.

Applying God's word is a vital part of one's relationship with God; it is the evidence that we are obeying him. The difficulty in applying the Bible is not with the Bible itself, but with the reader's inability to bridge the gap between the past and present, the conceptual and practical. When we don't or can't do this, spiritual dryness, shallowness, and indifference are the results.

The words of Scripture itself cry out to us, "But don't just listen to God's word. You must do what it says. Otherwise, you are only fooling yourselves" (James 1:22). The *Life Application Study Bible* helps us to obey God's word. Developed by an interdenominational team of pastors, scholars, family counselors, and a national organization dedicated to promoting God's word and spreading the gospel, the *Life Application Study Bible* took many years to complete. All the work was reviewed by several renowned theologians under the directorship of Dr. Kenneth Kantzer.

The *Life Application Study Bible* does what a good resource Bible should: It helps you understand the context of a passage, gives important background and historical information, explains difficult words and phrases, and helps you see the interrelationship of Scripture. But it does much more. The *Life Application Study Bible* goes deeper into God's word, helping you discover the timeless truth being communicated, see the relevance for your life, and make a personal application. While some study Bibles attempt application, over 75 percent of this Bible is application oriented. The notes answer the questions "So what?" and "What does this passage mean to me, my family, my friends, my job, my neighborhood, my church, my country?"

Imagine reading a familiar passage of Scripture and gaining fresh insight, as if it were the first time you had ever read it. How much richer your life would be if you left each Bible reading with a new perspective and a small change for the better. A small change every day adds up to a changed life—and that is the very purpose of Scripture.

WHAT IS APPLICATION?

The best way to define application is to first determine what it is *not*. Application is *not* just accumulating knowledge. Accumulating knowledge helps us discover and understand facts and concepts, but it stops there. History is filled with philosophers who knew what the Bible said but failed to apply it to their lives, keeping them from believing and changing. Many think that understanding is the end goal of Bible study, but it is really only the beginning.

Application is *not* just illustration. Illustration only tells us how someone else handled a similar situation. While we may empathize with that person, we still have little direction for our personal situation.

Application is *not* just making a passage "relevant." Making the Bible relevant only helps us to see that the same lessons that were true in Bible times are true today; it does not show us how to apply them to the problems and pressures of our individual lives.

What, then, is application? Application begins by knowing and understanding God's word and its timeless truths. *But you cannot stop there*. If you do, God's word may not change your life, and it may become dull, difficult, tedious, and tiring. A good application focuses the truth of God's word, shows the reader what to do about what is being read, and motivates the reader to respond to what God is teaching. All three are essential to application.

Application is putting into practice what we already know (see Mark 4:24 and Hebrews 5:14) and answering the question "So what?" by confronting us with the right questions and motivating us to take action (see 1 John 2:5-6 and James 2:26). Application is deeply personal—unique for each individual. It makes a relevant truth a personal truth and involves developing a strategy and action plan to live your life in harmony with the Bible. It is the biblical "how to" of life.

You may ask, "How can your application notes be relevant to my life?" Each application note has three parts: (1) an *explanation*, which ties the note directly to the Scripture passage and sets up the truth that is being taught; (2) the *bridge*, which explains the timeless truth and makes it relevant for today; (3) the *application*, which shows you how to take the timeless truth and apply it to your personal situation. No note, by itself, can apply Scripture directly to your life. It can only teach, direct, lead, guide, inspire, recommend, and urge. It can give you the resources and direction you need to apply the Bible, but only you can take these resources and put them into practice.

A good note, therefore, should not only give you knowledge and understanding but point you to application. Before you buy any kind of resource study Bible, you should evaluate the notes and ask the following questions: (1) Does the note contain enough information to help me understand the point of the Scripture passage? (2) Does the note assume I know more than I do? (3) Does the note avoid denominational bias? (4) Do the notes touch most of life's experiences? (5) Does the note help me apply God's word?

NOTES

In addition to providing the reader with many application notes, the *Life Application Study Bible* also offers several kinds of explanatory notes, which help the reader understand culture, history, context, difficult-to-understand passages, background, places, theological concepts, and the relationship of various passages in Scripture to other passages.

BOOK INTRODUCTIONS

Each book introduction is divided into several easy-to-find parts:

Timeline. A guide that puts the Bible book into its historical setting. It lists the key events and the dates when they occurred.

Vital Statistics. A list of straight facts about the book—those pieces of information you need to know at a glance.

Overview. A summary of the book with general lessons and applications that can be learned from the book as a whole.

Blueprint. The outline of the book. It is printed in easy-to-understand language and is designed for easy memorization. To the right of each main heading is a key lesson that is taught in that particular section.

Megathemes. A section that gives the main themes of the Bible book, explains their significance, and then tells you why they are still important for us today.

Map. If included, this shows the key places found in that book and retells the story of the book from a geographical point of view.

OUTLINE

The *Life Application Study Bible* has a new, custom-made outline that was designed specifically from an application point of view. Several unique features should be noted:

1. To avoid confusion and to aid memory work, the book outline has only three levels for headings. Main outline heads are marked with a capital letter. Subheads are marked by a number. Minor explanatory heads have no letter or number.

2. Each main outline head marked by a letter also has a brief paragraph below it summarizing the Bible text and offering a general application.

3. Parallel passages are listed where they apply.

PERSONALITY PROFILES

Among the unique features of this Bible are the profiles of key Bible people, including their strengths and weaknesses, greatest accomplishments and mistakes, and key lessons from their lives.

MAPS
The *Life Application Study Bible* has a thorough and comprehensive Bible atlas built right into the book. There are two kinds of maps: a book-introduction map, telling the story of the book, and thumbnail maps in the notes, plotting most geographic movements.

CHARTS AND DIAGRAMS
Many charts and diagrams are included to help the reader better visualize difficult concepts or relationships. Most charts not only present the needed information but show the significance of the information as well.

CROSS-REFERENCES
An updated, exhaustive cross-reference system in the margins of the Bible text helps the reader find related passages quickly.

TEXTUAL NOTES
Directly related to the text of the New Living Translation, the textual notes provide explanations on certain wording in the translation, alternate translations, and information about readings in the ancient manuscripts.

HIGHLIGHTED NOTES
In each Bible study lesson, you will be asked to read specific notes as part of your preparation. These notes have each been highlighted by a bullet (•) so that you can find them easily.

2 CORINTHIANS

VITAL STATISTICS

PURPOSE:
To affirm Paul's ministry, defend his authority as an apostle, and refute the false teachers in Corinth

AUTHOR:
Paul

ORIGINAL AUDIENCE:
The church in Corinth

DATE WRITTEN:
Approximately A.D. 55–57, from Macedonia

SETTING:
Paul had already written three letters to the Corinthians (two are now lost). In 1 Corinthians (the second of these letters), he used strong words to correct and teach. Most of the church had responded in the right spirit; there were, however, those who were denying Paul's authority and questioning his motives.

KEY VERSE:
"So we are Christ's ambassadors; God is making his appeal through us. We speak for Christ when we plead 'Come back to God!'" (5:20)

KEY PEOPLE:
Paul, Timothy, Titus, false teachers

KEY PLACES:
Corinth, Jerusalem

SPECIAL FEATURES:
This is an intensely personal and autobiographical letter.

SLITHERING through the centuries, the serpent whispers his smooth-tongued promises, beguiling, deceiving, and tempting—urging men and women to reject God and to follow Satan. Satan's emissaries have been many—false prophets contradicting God's ancient spokesmen, "pious" leaders hurling blasphemous accusations, and heretical teachers infiltrating churches. And the deception continues. Our world is filled with cults, "isms," and ideologies, all claiming to provide the way to God.

Paul constantly struggled with those who would mislead God's people, and he poured his life into spreading the Good News to the uttermost parts of the world. During three missionary trips and other travels, he proclaimed Christ, made converts, and established churches. But often young believers were easy prey for false teachers, who were a constant threat to the gospel and the early church. So Paul had to spend much time warning and correcting these new Christians.

The church at Corinth was weak. Surrounded by idolatry and immorality, they struggled with their Christian faith and life-style. Through personal visits and letters, Paul tried to instruct them in the faith, resolve their conflicts, and solve some of their problems. First Corinthians was sent to deal with specific moral issues in the church and to answer questions about sex, marriage, and tender consciences. That letter confronted the issues directly and was well received by most. But there were false teachers who denied Paul's authority and slandered him. Paul then wrote 2 Corinthians to defend his position and to denounce those who were twisting the truth.

Second Corinthians must have been a difficult letter for Paul to write because he had to list his credentials as an apostle. Paul was reluctant to do so as a humble servant of Christ, but he knew it was necessary. Paul also knew that most of the believers in Corinth had taken his previous words to heart and were beginning to mature in their faith. He affirmed their commitment to Christ.

Second Corinthians begins with Paul reminding his readers of (1) his relationship to them—Paul had always been honest and straightforward with them (1:12–14), (2) his itinerary—he was planning to visit them again (1:15—2:2), and (3) his previous letter (2:3–11). Paul then moves directly to the subject of false teachers (2:17), and he reviews his ministry among the Corinthians to demonstrate the validity of his message and to urge them not to turn away from the truth (3:1—7:16).

Paul next turns to the issue of collecting money for the poor Christians in Jerusalem. He tells them how others have given, and he urges them to show their love in a tangible way as well (8:1—9:15). Paul then gives a strong defense of his authority as a genuine apostle while pointing out the deceptive influence of the false apostles (10:1—13:10).

As you read this intensely personal letter, listen to Paul's words of love and exhortation, and be committed to the truth of God's Word and prepared to reject all false teaching.

THE BLUEPRINT

1. Paul explains his actions
   (1:1—2:11)
2. Paul defends his ministry
   (2:12—7:16)
3. Paul defends the collection
   (8:1—9:15)
4. Paul defends his authority
   (10:1—13:14)

In responding to the attacks on his character and authority, Paul explains the nature of Christian ministry and, as an example, openly shares about his ministry. This is an important letter for all who wish to be involved in any kind of Christian ministry, because it has much to teach us about how we should handle our ministries today. Like Paul, those involved in ministry should be blameless, sincere, confident, caring, open, and willing to suffer for the sake of Christ.

MEGATHEMES

THEME	EXPLANATION	IMPORTANCE
Trials	Paul experienced great suffering, persecution, and opposition in his ministry. He even struggled with a personal weakness—a "thorn" in the flesh. Through it all, Paul affirmed God's faithfulness.	God is faithful. His strength is sufficient for any trial. When trials come, they keep us from pride and teach us dependence on God. He comforts us so we can comfort others.
Church Discipline	Paul defends his role in church discipline. Neither immorality nor false teaching could be ignored. The church was to be neither too lax nor too severe in administering discipline. The church was to restore the corrected person when he or she repented.	The goal of all discipline in the church should be correction, not vengeance. For churches to be effective, they must confront and solve problems, not ignore them. In everything, we must act in love.
Hope	To encourage the Corinthians as they faced trials, Paul reminded them that they would receive new bodies in heaven. This would be a great victory in contrast to their present suffering.	To know we will receive new bodies offers us hope. No matter what adversity we face, we can keep going. Our faithful service will result in triumph.
Giving	Paul organized a collection of funds for the poor in the Jerusalem church. Many of the Asian churches gave money. Paul explains and defends his beliefs about giving, and he urges the Corinthians to follow through on their previous commitment.	Like the Corinthians, we should follow through on our financial commitments. Our giving must be generous, sacrificial, well planned, and based on need. Our generosity not only helps those in need but enables them to thank God.
Sound Doctrine	False teachers were challenging Paul's ministry and authority as an apostle. Paul asserts his authority in order to preserve correct Christian doctrine. His sincerity, his love for Christ, and his concern for the people were his defense.	We should share Paul's concern for correct teaching in our churches. But in so doing, we must share his motivation—love for Christ and people—and his sincerity.

1. Paul explains his actions

Greetings from Paul

1 This letter is from Paul, chosen by the will of God to be an apostle of Christ Jesus, and from our brother Timothy.

I am writing to God's church in Corinth and to all of his holy people throughout Greece.*

²May God our Father and the Lord Jesus Christ give you grace and peace.

1:1
1 Cor 1:1
2 Cor 1:19
Eph 1:1

1:2
Rom 1:7

God Offers Comfort to All

³All praise to God, the Father of our Lord Jesus Christ. God is our merciful Father and the source of all comfort. ⁴He comforts us in all our troubles so that we can comfort others. When they are troubled, we will be able to give them the same comfort God has given us. ⁵For the more we suffer for Christ, the more God will shower us with his comfort through Christ. ⁶Even when we are weighed down with troubles, it is for your comfort and salvation! For when we ourselves are comforted, we will certainly comfort you. Then you can patiently endure the same things we suffer. ⁷We are confident that as you share in our sufferings, you will also share in the comfort God gives us.

1:3
Eph 1:3
1 Pet 1:3

1:4
Isa 51:12; 66:13
2 Cor 7:6

1:5
2 Cor 4:10
Phil 3:10
Col 1:24

1:6
2 Cor 4:15

⁸We think you ought to know, dear brothers and sisters,* about the trouble we went through in the province of Asia. We were crushed and overwhelmed beyond our ability to endure, and we thought we would never live through it. ⁹In fact, we expected to die. But as a result, we stopped relying on ourselves and learned to rely only on God, who raises the dead. ¹⁰And he did rescue us from mortal danger, and he will rescue us again. We have placed our

1:9
Jer 17:5, 7

1:10
2 Tim 4:18
2 Pet 2:9

1:1 Greek *Achaia*, the southern region of the Greek peninsula.   **1:8** Greek *brothers*.

• **1:1** Paul visited Corinth on his second missionary journey and founded a church there (Acts 18:1ff). He later wrote several letters to the believers in Corinth, two of which are included in the Bible. Paul's first letter to the Corinthians is lost (1 Corinthians 5:9-11), his second letter to them is our book of 1 Corinthians, his third letter is lost (2:6-9; 7:12), and his fourth letter is our book of 2 Corinthians. Second Corinthians was written less than a year after 1 Corinthians.

Paul wrote 1 Corinthians to deal with divisions in the church. When his advice was not taken and their problems weren't solved, Paul visited Corinth a second time. That visit was painful both for Paul and for the church (2:1). He then planned a third visit but delayed it and wrote 2 Corinthians instead. After writing 2 Corinthians, Paul visited Corinth once more (Acts 20:2, 3).

1:1 Paul had great respect for Timothy (see also Philippians 2:19, 20; 1 Timothy 1:2), one of his traveling companions (Acts 16:1-3). Timothy had accompanied Paul to Corinth on his second missionary journey, and Paul had recently sent him there to minister (1 Corinthians 4:17; 16:10). Timothy's report to Paul about the crisis in the Corinthian church prompted Paul to make an unplanned visit to the church to deal with the problem in person (see 2:1). For more information on Timothy, see his Profile in 1 Timothy 2, p. 2059.

• **1:1** The Romans had made Corinth the capital of Achaia (the southern half of present-day Greece). The city was a flourishing trade center because of its seaport. With the thousands of merchants and sailors who disembarked there each year, it had developed a reputation as one of the most immoral cities in the ancient world; its many pagan temples encouraged the practice of sexual immorality along with idol worship. In fact, the Greek word "to Corinthianize" came to mean "to practice sexual immorality." A Christian church in the city would face many pressures and conflicts. For more information on Corinth, see the first note on 1 Corinthians 1:2.

• **1:3-5** Many think that when God comforts us, our troubles should go away. But if that were always so, people would turn to God only out of a desire to be relieved of pain and not out of love for him. We must understand that being "comforted" can

also mean receiving strength, encouragement, and hope to deal with our troubles. The more we suffer, the more comfort God gives us. If you are feeling overwhelmed, allow God to comfort you. Remember that every trial you endure will help you comfort other people who are suffering similar troubles.

• **1:5** Suffering for Christ refers to those afflictions we experience as we serve Christ. At the same time, Christ suffers with his people, since they are united with him. In Acts 9:4, 5 Christ asked Paul why he was persecuting him. This implies that Christ suffered with the early Christians when they were persecuted.

• **1:6, 7** Paul had a radically different view of suffering. Suffering—especially trials and discomfort associated with the advancement of Christ's Kingdom—is God's way of allowing Christians to become more like Jesus, to suffer for the gospel just as Jesus suffered for it (Philippians 1:29; 3:10). Peter agreed with Paul: Christians should rejoice when they suffer, for in their own suffering they will in some small way experience what it meant for Jesus to suffer for their sins (1 Peter 4:12, 13).

In addition to drawing people closer to Christ, suffering can also help them grow in their faith. God uses suffering to improve his people and shape them into better Christians. In fact, suffering should be thought of as the necessary pain that accompanies spiritual growth. In Romans, Paul noted that suffering produces perseverance, which, in turn produces Christian character (Romans 5:3, 4; see also James 1:3, 4; 2 Peter 1:6; Revelation 2:2, 19). This passage highlights another benefit to suffering: It teaches the sufferer how to encourage others who are also suffering.

1:8-10 Paul does not give details about their hardships in Asia, although his accounts of all three missionary journeys record many difficult trials he faced (Acts 13:2–14:28; Acts 15:40–21:17). He does write that they felt that they were going to die and realized that they could do nothing to help themselves—they simply had to rely on God.

• **1:8-10** We often depend on our own skills and abilities when life seems easy and only turn to God when we feel unable to help ourselves. But as we realize our own powerlessness without him and our need for his constant help in our lives, we come to depend on him more and more. God is our source of power, and we receive his help by keeping in touch with him. With this attitude of dependence, problems will drive us to God rather than away from him. Learn how to rely on God daily.

1:11
Rom 15:30
2 Cor 4:15
Phil 1:19

confidence in him, and he will continue to rescue us. 11And you are helping us by praying for us. Then many people will give thanks because God has graciously answered so many prayers for our safety.

Paul's Change of Plans

1:12
Acts 23:1
1 Cor 1:17
2 Cor 2:17; 4:15

12 We can say with confidence and a clear conscience that we have lived with a God-given holiness* and sincerity in all our dealings. We have depended on God's grace, not on our own human wisdom. That is how we have conducted ourselves before the world, and especially toward you. 13Our letters have been straightforward, and there is nothing written between the lines and nothing you can't understand. I hope someday you will fully understand

1:14
2 Cor 5:12
Phil 2:16

us, 14 even if you don't understand us now. Then on the day when the Lord Jesus* returns, you will be proud of us in the same way we are proud of you.

1:15
Rom 1:11-13

1:16
Acts 19:21
1 Cor 16:5-6

15Since I was so sure of your understanding and trust, I wanted to give you a double blessing by visiting you twice—16first on my way to Macedonia and again when I returned from Macedonia.* Then you could send me on my way to Judea.

1:17
2 Cor 5:16

1:19
Acts 18:5
Heb 13:8

17 You may be asking why I changed my plan. Do you think I make my plans carelessly? Do you think I am like people of the world who say "Yes" when they really mean "No"? 18As surely as God is faithful, our word to you does not waver between "Yes" and "No." 19For Jesus Christ, the Son of God, does not waver between "Yes" and "No." He is the one whom Silas,* Timothy, and I preached to you, and as God's ultimate "Yes," he always does what he says.

1:20
Rom 15:8-9
Rev 3:14

20For all of God's promises have been fulfilled in Christ with a resounding "Yes!" And through Christ, our "Amen" (which means "Yes") ascends to God for his glory.

1:12 Some manuscripts read *honesty.*   **1:14** Some manuscripts read *our Lord Jesus.*   **1:16** *Macedonia* was in the northern region of Greece.   **1:19** Greek *Silvanus.*

DIFFERENCES BETWEEN 1 AND 2 CORINTHIANS

The two letters to the Corinthian church that we find in the Bible are very different, with different tones and focuses.

1 Corinthians/Practical	*2 Corinthians*/Personal
Focuses on the character of the Corinthian church	Focuses on Paul as he bares his soul and tells of his love for the Corinthian church
Deals with questions on marriage, freedom, spiritual gifts, and order in the church	Deals with the problem of false teachers, whereby Paul defends his authority and the truth of his message
Paul instructs in matters concerning the church's well-being	Paul gives his testimony because he knows that acceptance of his advice is vital to the church's well-being
Contains advice to help the church combat the pagan influences in the wicked city of Corinth	Contains testimony to help the church combat the havoc caused by false teachers

---

1:11 Paul requested prayer for himself and his companions as they traveled to spread God's message. Pray for pastors, teachers, missionaries, and others who are spreading the Good News. Satan will challenge anyone making a real difference for God.

1:12-14 Paul knew the importance of honesty and sincerity in word and action, especially in a situation as in Corinth, where constructive criticism was necessary. So Paul did not come with impressive human wisdom. God wants us to be real and transparent in all our relationships. If we aren't, we may end up lowering ourselves to spreading rumors, gossiping, and second-guessing.

• **1:15-17** Paul had recently made a brief, unscheduled visit to Corinth that was very painful for him and the church (see 2:1). After that visit, he told the church when he would return. But Paul changed his original travel plans. Instead of sailing from Ephesus to Corinth before going to Macedonia, he traveled from Ephesus directly to Macedonia, where he wrote a letter to the Corinthians that caused him much anguish and them much sorrow (7:8, 9). He had made his original plans, thinking that the church would have solved its problems. When the time came for Paul's scheduled trip to Corinth, however, the crisis had not been fully resolved (although progress was being made in some areas; 7:11-16). So he wrote a letter instead (2:3, 4; 7:8) because another visit might

have only made matters worse. Thus, Paul stayed away from Corinth because he was concerned over the church's unity, not because he was fickle.

• **1:17-20** Paul's change of plans caused some of his accusers to say that he couldn't be trusted, hoping to undermine his authority. Paul said that he was not the type of person to say yes when he meant no. Paul explained that it was not indecision but concern for their feelings that forced him to change his plans. The reason for his trip—to bring joy (1:24)—could not be accomplished with the present crisis. Paul didn't want to visit them only to rebuke them severely (1:23). Just as the Corinthians could trust God to keep his promises, they could trust Paul as God's representative to keep his. He would still visit them, but at a better time.

1:19, 20 Instead of defending himself, Paul reminded the Corinthians of God's faithfulness. There was no duplicity in God. His promises would be fulfilled. There would be no wavering between "yes" and "no." Jesus Christ was the premier example of this. "All of God's promises have been fulfilled in Christ with a resounding 'yes!'" Jesus is the embodiment of God's faithfulness. Because Jesus Christ is faithful, Paul (a messenger appointed by Jesus) would also be faithful in his ministry.

²¹It is God who enables us, along with you, to stand firm for Christ. He has commissioned us, ²²and he has identified us as his own by placing the Holy Spirit in our hearts as the first installment that guarantees everything he has promised us.

²³Now I call upon God as my witness that I am telling the truth. The reason I didn't return to Corinth was to spare you from a severe rebuke. ²⁴But that does not mean we want to dominate you by telling you how to put your faith into practice. We want to work together with you so you will be full of joy, for it is by your own faith that you stand firm.

2 So I decided that I would not bring you grief with another painful visit. ²For if I cause you grief, who will make me glad? Certainly not someone I have grieved. ³That is why I wrote to you as I did, so that when I do come, I won't be grieved by the very ones who ought to give me the greatest joy. Surely you all know that my joy comes from your being joyful. ⁴I wrote that letter in great anguish, with a troubled heart and many tears. I didn't want to grieve you, but I wanted to let you know how much love I have for you.

Forgiveness for the Sinner

⁵I am not overstating it when I say that the man who caused all the trouble hurt all of you more than he hurt me. ⁶Most of you opposed him, and that was punishment enough. ⁷Now, however, it is time to forgive and comfort him. Otherwise he may be overcome by discouragement. ⁸So I urge you now to reaffirm your love for him.

⁹I wrote to you as I did to test you and see if you would fully comply with my instructions. ¹⁰When you forgive this man, I forgive him, too. And when I forgive whatever needs to be forgiven, I do so with Christ's authority for your benefit, ¹¹so that Satan will not outsmart us. For we are familiar with his evil schemes.

¹²When I came to the city of Troas to preach the Good News of Christ, the Lord opened a door of opportunity for me. ¹³But I had no peace of mind because my dear brother Titus hadn't yet arrived with a report from you. So I said good-bye and went on to Macedonia to find him.

1:21
1 Jn 2:20, 27
1:22
2 Cor 5:5
Eph 1:13-14; 4:30
1:23
1 Cor 4:21
1:24
1 Cor 15:1

2:1
1 Cor 4:21
2 Cor 12:21
2:2
2 Cor 7:8
2:4
2 Cor 2:9; 7:8, 12

2:5
1 Cor 5:1-2
2 Cor 7:11
2:7
Gal 6:1
Eph 4:32
2:11
2 Cor 4:4
1 Pet 5:8
2:12
Acts 14:27
2 Cor 4:3
2:13
2 Cor 7:5-6

1:21, 22 The Holy Spirit guarantees that we belong to God and will receive all his benefits (Ephesians 1:13, 14). The Holy Spirit guarantees that salvation is ours now, and that we will receive so much more when Christ returns. The great comfort and power the Holy Spirit gives in this life is a foretaste or down payment ("first installment") of the benefits of our eternal life in God's presence. With the privilege of belonging to God comes the responsibility of identifying ourselves as his faithful servants. Don't be ashamed to let others know that you are his.

1:23 The Corinthian church had written to Paul with questions about their faith (see 1 Corinthians 7:1). In response, Paul had written 1 Corinthians. But the church did not follow his instructions.

Paul had planned to visit them again, but instead, he wrote a letter that caused sorrow (7:8, 9) but also caused them to change their ways. He had not wanted to visit and repeat the same advice for the same problems. He wrote the emotional letter to encourage them to follow the advice that he had already given in previous letters and visits.

1:24 Standing firm is not a way to be saved but the evidence that a person is really committed to Jesus. Endurance is not a means to earn salvation; it is the by-product of a truly devoted life. Endurance grows out of commitment to Jesus Christ. In Matthew 10:22, Jesus predicted that his followers would be severely persecuted by those who hated what he stood for. In the midst of terrible persecutions, however, they could have hope, knowing that salvation was theirs. Times of trial serve to sift true Christians from false or fair-weather Christians. When you are pressured to give up and turn your back on Christ, don't do it. Remember the benefits of standing firm and continue to live for Christ.

● **2:1** Paul's phrase "another painful visit" indicates that he had already made one difficult trip to Corinth (see the notes on 1:1; 1:15-17) since founding the church. Paul had gone there to deal with those in the church who had been attacking and undermining his authority as an apostle of Jesus Christ, thus confusing other believers.

2:3 Paul's last letter, referred to here, was not the book of 1 Corinthians, but a letter written between 1 and 2 Corinthians,

just after his unplanned, painful visit (2:1). Paul refers to this letter again in 7:8.

2:4 Paul did not enjoy reprimanding his friends and fellow believers, but he cared enough about the Corinthians to confront them with their wrongdoing. Proverbs 27:6 says: "Wounds from a sincere friend are better than many kisses from an enemy." Sometimes our friends make choices that we know are wrong. If we ignore their behavior and let them continue in it, we won't be showing love to them. We show love by honestly sharing our concerns in order to help these friends be their very best for God. When we don't make any move to help, we show that we are more concerned about being well liked than about what will happen to them.

2:5-11 Paul explained that it was time to forgive the man who had been punished by the church and had subsequently repented. He needed forgiveness, acceptance, and comfort. Satan would gain an advantage if they permanently separated this man from the congregation rather than forgiving and restoring him. This may have been the man who had required the disciplinary action described in 1 Corinthians 5, or he may have been the chief opponent of Paul who had caused him anguish (2:1-11). The sorrowful letter had finally brought about the repentance of the Corinthians (7:8-14), and their discipline of the man had led to his repentance. Church discipline should seek restoration. Two mistakes in church discipline should be avoided: being too lenient and not correcting mistakes, or being too harsh and not forgiving the sinner. There is a time to confront and a time to comfort.

2:11 We use church discipline to help keep the church pure and to help wayward people repent. But Satan tries to harm the church by tempting it to use discipline in an unforgiving way. This causes those exercising discipline to become proud of their purity, and it causes the person who is being disciplined to become bitter and perhaps leave the church. We must remember that our purpose in discipline is to *restore* a person to the fellowship, not to destroy him or her. We must be cautious that personal anger is not vented under the guise of church discipline.

2:13 Titus was a Greek convert whom Paul greatly loved and trusted (the book of Titus is a letter that Paul wrote to him). Titus

2. Paul defends his ministry

Ministers of the New Covenant

14But thank God! He has made us his captives and continues to lead us along in Christ's triumphal procession. Now he uses us to spread the knowledge of Christ everywhere, like a sweet perfume. 15Our lives are a Christ-like fragrance rising up to God. But this fragrance is perceived differently by those who are being saved and by those who are perishing. 16To those who are perishing, we are a dreadful smell of death and doom. But to those who are being saved, we are a life-giving perfume. And who is adequate for such a task as this?

17You see, we are not like the many hucksters* who preach for personal profit. We preach the word of God with sincerity and with Christ's authority, knowing that God is watching us.

2:15
1 Cor 1:18

2:16
Luke 2:34
2 Cor 3:5-6

2:17
2 Cor 1:12; 12:19

2:17 Some manuscripts read *the rest of the hucksters.*

PAUL SEARCHES FOR TITUS
Paul had searched for Titus, hoping to meet him in Troas and receive news about the Corinthian church. When he did not find Titus in Troas, he went on to Macedonia (2:13), most likely to Philippi, where he found Titus.

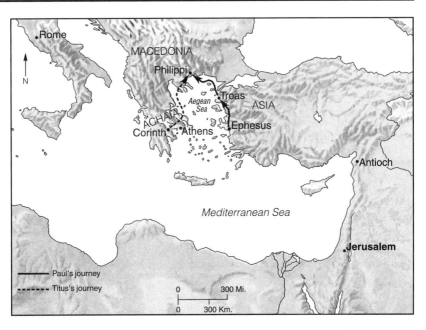

Paul's journey
Titus's journey

0   300 Mi.
0   300 Km.

was one of the men responsible for collecting the money for the poverty-stricken Jerusalem church (8:6). Paul may also have sent Titus with the sorrowful letter. On his way to Macedonia, Paul was supposed to meet Titus in Troas. When Paul didn't find him there, he was worried for Titus's safety and left Troas to search for him in Macedonia. There Paul found him (7:6), and the good news that Paul received (7:8-16) led to this letter. Paul would send Titus back to Corinth with this letter (8:16, 17).

2:14ff In the middle of discussing his unscheduled trip to Macedonia, Paul thanked God for his ministry, his relationship with the Corinthian believers, and the way God had used him to help others wherever he went, despite difficulties (2:14–7:4). In 7:5, Paul resumed his story of his trip to Macedonia.

2:14-16 In a Roman triumphal procession, the Roman general would display his treasures and captives amidst a cloud of incense burned for the gods. To the victors, the aroma was sweet; to the captives in the parade, it was the smell of slavery and death. When Christians preach the Good News, it is good news to some and repulsive news to others. Believers recognize the life-giving fragrance of the message. To nonbelievers, however, it smells foul, like death—their own.

• **2:16, 17** Paul asks "who is adequate" for the task of representing Christ? Our adequacy is always from God (1 Corinthians

15:10; 2 Corinthians 3:5). He has already commissioned and sent us (see Matthew 28:18-20). He has given us the Holy Spirit to enable us to speak with Christ's power. He keeps his eye on us, protecting us as we work for him. As we realize that God has equipped us, we can overcome our feelings of inadequacy. Serving Christ, therefore, requires that we focus on what he can do through us, not on what we can't do by ourselves.

2:17 Some preachers in Paul's day were "hucksters," preaching without understanding God's message or caring about what happened to their listeners. They weren't concerned about furthering God's Kingdom—they just wanted money. Today there are still preachers and teachers who care only about money and not about truth. Those who truly speak for God should teach God's Word with sincerity and integrity and should never preach for selfish reasons (1 Timothy 6:5-10).

3 Are we beginning to praise ourselves again? Are we like others, who need to bring you letters of recommendation, or who ask you to write such letters on their behalf? Surely not! ²The only letter of recommendation we need is you yourselves. Your lives are a letter written in our* hearts; everyone can read it and recognize our good work among you. ³Clearly, you are a letter from Christ showing the result of our ministry among you. This "letter" is written not with pen and ink, but with the Spirit of the living God. It is carved not on tablets of stone, but on human hearts.

⁴We are confident of all this because of our great trust in God through Christ. ⁵It is not that we think we are qualified to do anything on our own. Our qualification comes from God. ⁶He has enabled us to be ministers of his new covenant. This is a covenant not of written laws, but of the Spirit. The old written covenant ends in death; but under the new covenant, the Spirit gives life.

The Glory of the New Covenant

⁷The old way,* with laws etched in stone, led to death, though it began with such glory that the people of Israel could not bear to look at Moses' face. For his face shone with the glory of God, even though the brightness was already fading away. ⁸Shouldn't we expect far greater glory under the new way, now that the Holy Spirit is giving life? ⁹If the old way, which brings condemnation, was glorious, how much more glorious is the new way, which makes us right with God! ¹⁰In fact, that first glory was not glorious at all compared with the overwhelming glory of the new way. ¹¹So if the old way, which has been replaced, was glorious, how much more glorious is the new, which remains forever!

¹²Since this new way gives us such confidence, we can be very bold. ¹³We are not like Moses, who put a veil over his face so the people of Israel would not see the glory, even though it was destined to fade away. ¹⁴But the people's minds were hardened, and to this day whenever the old covenant is being read, the same veil covers their minds so they cannot understand the truth. And this veil can be removed only by believing in Christ. ¹⁵Yes, even today when they read Moses' writings, their hearts are covered with that veil, and they do not understand.

¹⁶But whenever someone turns to the Lord, the veil is taken away. ¹⁷For the Lord is the

3:2 Some manuscripts read *your.*   **3:7** Or *ministry;* also in 3:8, 9, 10, 11, 12.

3:1	Acts 18:27 2 Cor 5:12; 10:12
3:2	1 Cor 9:2
3:3	Exod 24:12; 31:18; 32:15-16 Prov 3:3 Jer 31:33 Ezek 36:26
3:5	1 Cor 15:10 2 Cor 2:16
3:6	Jer 31:31 Luke 22:20 Rom 2:27; 7:6; 8:2 Heb 8:8-13
3:7	Exod 34:29-35
3:9	Deut 27:26 Rom 1:17; 3:21
3:10-11	Exod 34:29-30 John 17:10, 22
3:13	Exod 34:33-35
3:14	Acts 13:15 Rom 11:7-8 2 Cor 4:4
3:16	Isa 25:7 Rom 11:23
3:17	Gal 4:6-7

3:1-3 Some false teachers had started carrying forged letters of recommendation to authenticate their authority. In no uncertain terms, Paul stated that he needed no such letters. The believers to whom Paul and his companions had preached were enough of a recommendation. Paul did use letters of introduction, however, many times. He wrote them on behalf of Phoebe (Romans 16:1, 2) and Timothy (1 Corinthians 16:10, 11). These letters helped Paul's trusted companions and friends find a welcome in various churches.

• **3:3** Paul uses powerful imagery from famous Old Testament passages predicting the promised day of new hearts and new beginnings for God's people (see Jeremiah 31:33; Ezekiel 11:19; 36:26). No human being can take credit for this process of conversion. It is the work of God's Spirit. We do not become believers by following some manual or using some technique. Our conversion is a result of God's implanting his Spirit in our heart, giving us new power to live for him.

• **3:4, 5** Paul was not boasting; he gave God the credit for all his accomplishments. While the false teachers boasted of their own power and success, Paul expressed his humility before God. No one can claim to be adequate without God's help. No one is competent to carry out the responsibilities of God's calling in his or her own strength. Without the Holy Spirit's enabling, our natural talent can carry us only so far. As Christ's witnesses, we need the character and special strength that only God gives.

• **3:6** "The old written covenant ends in death; but under the new covenant, the Spirit gives life" means that trying to be saved by keeping the Old Testament laws will end in death. Only by believing in the Lord Jesus Christ can a person receive eternal life through the Holy Spirit. No one but Jesus has ever fulfilled the law perfectly; thus, the whole world is condemned to death. The law makes people realize their sin, but it cannot give life. Under the new covenant, which means promise or agreement, eternal life comes from

the Holy Spirit. The Spirit gives new life to all who believe in Christ. The moral law (Ten Commandments) still points out sin and shows us how to obey God, but forgiveness comes only through the grace and mercy of Christ (see Romans 7:10–8:2).

3:7-11 Paul recalled the stone tablets on which God had written the old covenant—calling it "the old way." He identified the law, although leading to death, as nonetheless glorious because it was God's provision and proof of his intervention in the life of his people. But that which was summarized on stone is nowhere near as glorious as what came with "the new way"—life in the Holy Spirit. The Holy Spirit was present at the creation of the world as one of the agents in the origin of life itself (Genesis 1:2). He is the power behind the rebirth of every Christian and the one who helps us live the Christian life. By his power, we will be transformed into Christ's perfect likeness when he returns. Thank God for the fact that the best is yet to be.

3:13-18 When Moses came down Mount Sinai with the Ten Commandments, his face glowed from being in God's presence (Exodus 34:29-35). Moses had to put on a veil to keep the people from being terrified by the brightness of his face and from seeing the radiance fade away. This veil illustrates the fading of the old system and the veiling of the people's minds because of their pride, hardness of heart, and refusal to repent. The veil kept them from understanding references to Christ in the Scriptures. When anyone becomes a Christian, the veil is taken away (3:16), giving eternal life and freedom from bondage. That person can then be like a mirror reflecting God's glory.

3:17 Those who were trying to be saved by keeping the Old Testament law were soon tied up in rules and ceremonies. But now, through the Holy Spirit, God provides freedom from sin and condemnation (Romans 8:1). When we trust Christ to save us, he removes our heavy burden of trying to please him and

3:18
Rom 8:29
2 Cor 4:4, 6

4:2
2 Cor 2:17
1 Thes 2:5

4:3
1 Cor 1:18
2 Cor 3:14

4:4
John 12:39-41
2 Cor 3:14
Col 1:15
Heb 1:3

4:5
1 Cor 9:19
2 Cor 1:24

4:6
Gen 1:3
Ps 36:9
John 8:12; 12:46
Eph 5:8, 14
1 Pet 2:9
2 Pet 1:19

4:7
2 Cor 5:1
2 Tim 2:20

4:8
2 Cor 7:5

4:9
Rom 8:35

4:10
Rom 8:17
1 Cor 15:31
Gal 6:17
Phil 3:10
Col 1:24
2 Tim 2:11
1 Pet 4:13

4:14
Acts 2:24
1 Thes 2:19

Spirit, and wherever the Spirit of the Lord is, there is freedom. 18So all of us who have had that veil removed can see and reflect the glory of the Lord. And the Lord—who is the Spirit—makes us more and more like him as we are changed into his glorious image.

Treasure in Fragile Clay Jars

4 Therefore, since God in his mercy has given us this new way,* we never give up. 2We reject all shameful deeds and underhanded methods. We don't try to trick anyone or distort the word of God. We tell the truth before God, and all who are honest know this.

3If the Good News we preach is hidden behind a veil, it is hidden only from people who are perishing. 4Satan, who is the god of this world, has blinded the minds of those who don't believe. They are unable to see the glorious light of the Good News. They don't understand this message about the glory of Christ, who is the exact likeness of God.

5You see, we don't go around preaching about ourselves. We preach that Jesus Christ is Lord, and we ourselves are your servants for Jesus' sake. 6For God, who said, "Let there be light in the darkness," has made this light shine in our hearts so we could know the glory of God that is seen in the face of Jesus Christ.

7We now have this light shining in our hearts, but we ourselves are like fragile clay jars containing this great treasure.* This makes it clear that our great power is from God, not from ourselves.

8We are pressed on every side by troubles, but we are not crushed. We are perplexed, but not driven to despair. 9We are hunted down, but never abandoned by God. We get knocked down, but we are not destroyed. 10Through suffering, our bodies continue to share in the death of Jesus so that the life of Jesus may also be seen in our bodies.

11Yes, we live under constant danger of death because we serve Jesus, so that the life of Jesus will be evident in our dying bodies. 12So we live in the face of death, but this has resulted in eternal life for you.

13But we continue to preach because we have the same kind of faith the psalmist had when he said, "I believed in God, so I spoke."* 14We know that God, who raised the Lord Jesus,* will

4:1 Or ministry.   **4:7** Greek We now have this treasure in clay jars.   **4:13** Ps 116:10.   **4:14** Some manuscripts read who raised Jesus.

---

our guilt for failing to do so. By trusting Christ we are loved, accepted, forgiven, and freed to live for him. "Wherever the Spirit of the Lord is, there is freedom."

• **3:18** The glory that the Spirit imparts to the believer is more excellent and lasts longer than the glory that Moses experienced. By gazing at the nature of God with unveiled minds, we can be more like him. In the Good News, we see the truth about Christ, and it transforms us morally as we understand and apply it. Through learning about Christ's life, we can understand how wonderful God is and what he is really like. As our knowledge deepens, the Holy Spirit helps us to change. Becoming Christlike is a progressive experience (see Romans 8:29; Galatians 4:19; Philippians 3:21; 1 John 3:2). The more closely we follow Christ, the more we will be like him.

4:2 Paul condemned those who twist God's Word. Preachers, teachers, and anyone else who talks about Jesus Christ must remember that they stand in God's presence—he hears every word. Many Christian ministers and leaders twist Scripture in their attempt to motivate audiences. Others take Scripture out of context to promote their own views. When you tell people about Christ, be careful not to distort the message to please your audience. Proclaim the truth of God's Word.

4:3, 4 The Good News is revealed to everyone, except to those who refuse to believe. Satan is "the god of this world." His work is to deceive, and he has blinded those who don't believe in Christ (see 11:14, 15). The allure of money, power, and pleasure blinds people to the light of Christ's Good News. Those who reject Christ and prefer their own pursuits have unknowingly made Satan their god.

4:5 The focus of Paul's preaching was Christ and not himself. When you witness, tell people about what Christ has done and not about your abilities and accomplishments. People must be introduced to Christ, not to you. And if you hear someone

preaching about himself or his own ideas rather than about Christ, beware—he is a false teacher.

4:5 Paul willingly served the Corinthian church even though the people must have deeply disappointed him. Serving people requires a sacrifice of time and personal desires. Being Christ's follower means serving others, even when they do not measure up to our expectations.

4:7 The supremely valuable message of salvation in Jesus Christ has been entrusted by God to frail and fallible human beings. Paul's focus, however, was not on the perishable container but on its priceless contents—God's power dwelling in us. Though we are "fragile, clay jars," God uses us to spread his Good News, and he gives us power to do his work. Knowing that the power is his, not ours, should keep us from pride and motivate us to keep daily contact with God, our power source. Our responsibility is to let people see God through us.

• **4:8-12** Paul reminds us that though we may think we are at the end of our rope, we are never at the end of our hope. Our perishable bodies are subject to sin and suffering, but God never abandons us. Because Christ has won the victory over death, we have eternal life. All our risks, humiliations, and trials are opportunities for Christ to demonstrate his power and presence in and through us. We must ask ourselves, "Could I handle the suffering and opposition that Paul did?" The success syndrome is a great enemy of effective ministry. From an earthly perspective, Paul was not very successful. Like Paul, we must carry out our ministry, looking to God for strength. When opposition, slander, or disappointment threaten to rob you of the victory, remember that no one can destroy what God has accomplished through you.

also raise us with Jesus and present us to himself together with you. ¹⁵All of this is for your benefit. And as God's grace reaches more and more people, there will be great thanksgiving, and God will receive more and more glory.

¹⁶That is why we never give up. Though our bodies are dying, our spirits are* being renewed every day. ¹⁷For our present troubles are small and won't last very long. Yet they produce for us a glory that vastly outweighs them and will last forever! ¹⁸So we don't look at the troubles we can see now; rather, we fix our gaze on things that cannot be seen. For the things we see now will soon be gone, but the things we cannot see will last forever.

New Bodies

5 For we know that when this earthly tent we live in is taken down (that is, when we die and leave this earthly body), we will have a house in heaven, an eternal body made for us by God himself and not by human hands. ²We grow weary in our present bodies, and we long to put on our heavenly bodies like new clothing. ³For we will put on heavenly bodies; we will not be spirits without bodies.* ⁴While we live in these earthly bodies, we groan and sigh, but it's not that we want to die and get rid of these bodies that clothe us. Rather, we want to put on our new bodies so that these dying bodies will be swallowed up by life. ⁵God himself has prepared us for this, and as a guarantee he has given us his Holy Spirit.

⁶So we are always confident, even though we know that as long as we live in these bodies we are not at home with the Lord. ⁷For we live by believing and not by seeing. ⁸Yes, we are fully confident, and we would rather be away from these earthly bodies, for then we will be at home with the Lord. ⁹So whether we are here in this body or away from this body, our goal is to please him. ¹⁰For we must all stand before Christ to be judged. We will each receive whatever we deserve for the good or evil we have done in this earthly body.

4:15
2 Cor 1:3-6
4:16
Eph 3:16
Col 3:10
4:17
Rom 8:17-18
1 Pet 1:6-7
4:18
Rom 8:24
2 Cor 5:7
5:1
1 Cor 15:47
2 Cor 4:7
2 Pet 1:13-14
5:2
Rom 8:23
1 Cor 15:53-54
5:4
1 Cor 15:53-54
5:5
Rom 8:23
2 Cor 1:22
Eph 1:13-14
5:7
1 Cor 13:12
5:8
Phil 1:23
5:10
Matt 16:27
Acts 10:42

4:16 Greek *our inner being is.*   **5:3** Greek *we will not be naked.*

● **4:15-18** Paul had faced suffering, trials, and distress as he preached the Good News. But he knew that they would one day be over, and he would obtain God's rest and rewards. As we face great troubles, it's easy to focus on the pain rather than on our ultimate goal. Just as athletes concentrate on the finish line and ignore their discomfort, we, too, must focus on the reward for our faith and the joy that lasts forever. No matter what happens to us in this life, we have the assurance of eternal life, when all suffering will end and all sorrow will flee away (Isaiah 35:10).

● **4:16** It is easy to lose heart and quit. We all have faced problems in our relationships or in our work that have caused us to think about giving up. Rather than quitting when persecution wore him down, Paul concentrated on the inner strength that came from the Holy Spirit (Ephesians 3:16). Don't let fatigue, pain, or criticism force you off the job. Renew your commitment to serving Christ. Don't forsake your eternal reward because of the intensity of today's pain. Your very weakness allows the resurrection power of Christ to strengthen you moment by moment.

● **4:17** Our troubles should not diminish our faith or disillusion us. We should realize that there is a purpose in our suffering. Problems and human limitations have several benefits: (1) They remind us of Christ's suffering for us; (2) they keep us from pride; (3) they cause us to look beyond this brief life; (4) they give us opportunities to prove our faith to others; and (5) they give God the opportunity to demonstrate his power. See your troubles as opportunities!

● **4:18** Our ultimate hope when we are experiencing terrible illness, persecution, or pain is the realization that this life is not all there is—there is life after death! Knowing that we will live forever with God in a place without sin and suffering can help us live above the pain that we face in this life.

5:1-10 Paul contrasts our earthly body and our future resurrection body. Paul clearly states that our present body makes us groan, but when we die we will not be spirits without bodies. We will have new bodies that will be perfect for our everlasting life.

Paul wrote as he did because the church at Corinth was surrounded by Greek culture, and many believers had difficulty with the concept of bodily resurrection because the Greeks did not believe in it. Most saw the afterlife as something that happened only to the soul, with the real person imprisoned in a physical body. They believed that at death the soul was released; there was no immortality for the body, and the soul enters an eternal state. But the Bible teaches that the body and soul are not permanently separated.

Paul describes our resurrected body in more detail in 1 Corinthians 15:46-58. We will still have personalities and recognizable characteristics in our resurrected body, but through Christ's work, our body will be better than we can imagine. The Bible does not tell us everything about our resurrected body, but we know that it will be perfect, without sickness, disease, or pain (see Philippians 3:21; Revelation 21:4).

5:4 Paul's knowledge that his dying body would be swallowed up by eternal life, is a universal hope. According to the writer of Ecclesiastes, God "has planted eternity in the human heart" (Ecclesiastes 3:11). Human beings have an innate sense of transcendence and longing for ultimate reality experienced only in the eternal presence of God. This spiritual desire is addressed by every world religion and cult and (at least secretly) desired by every person. What occurrences in daily life can provide you an opportunity to witness God's solution to this universal spiritual search? A baby's birth, a parent's death, or the death of a dream all can be springboards for sharing the hope you have in Christ. Spread the Good News!

● **5:5** The Holy Spirit is God's "guarantee" of what will come. His work in our lives today assures us that the healing process will be thoroughly completed in Christ's presence. Each time the Holy Spirit reminds you of Scripture, convicts you of sin, restrains you from selfish behavior, or prompts you to love, you have evidence that he is present. You have the Spirit within you beginning the transformation process. Whether you deal with aches and pains or even disabling limitations, trust God that his total renovation of your body and soul is in process.

● **5:6-8** Paul was not afraid to die because he was confident of spending eternity with Christ. Of course, facing the unknown may cause us anxiety, and leaving loved ones hurts deeply, but if we believe in Jesus Christ, we can share Paul's hope and confidence of eternal life with Christ. Death is only a prelude to eternal life with God. We will continue to live. Let this hope give you confidence and inspire you to faithful service.

5:9, 10 While eternal life is a free gift given on the basis of God's grace (Ephesians 2:8, 9), each of us will still be judged by Christ.

We Are God's Ambassadors

5:12
2 Cor 1:14; 3:1

5:14
Rom 6:6-7
Gal 2:20
Col 3:3

5:15
Rom 14:7-9

5:16
2 Cor 10:4

5:17
Isa 65:17
Gal 6:15
Rev 21:5

5:18
Rom 5:10

5:19
Rom 3:24; 4:8

5:20
Eph 6:20

5:21
Isa 53:6, 9
Jer 23:6
Gal 3:13
Heb 4:15; 7:26
1 Pet 2:22

6:1
1 Cor 3:9
2 Cor 5:20

6:2
†Isa 49:8

¹¹Because we understand our fearful responsibility to the Lord, we work hard to persuade others. God knows we are sincere, and I hope you know this, too. ¹²Are we commending ourselves to you again? No, we are giving you a reason to be proud of us,* so you can answer those who brag about having a spectacular ministry rather than having a sincere heart. ¹³If it seems we are crazy, it is to bring glory to God. And if we are in our right minds, it is for your benefit. ¹⁴Either way, Christ's love controls us.* Since we believe that Christ died for all, we also believe that we have all died to our old life.* ¹⁵He died for everyone so that those who receive his new life will no longer live for themselves. Instead, they will live for Christ, who died and was raised for them.

¹⁶So we have stopped evaluating others from a human point of view. At one time we thought of Christ merely from a human point of view. How differently we know him now! ¹⁷This means that anyone who belongs to Christ has become a new person. The old life is gone; a new life has begun!

¹⁸And all of this is a gift from God, who brought us back to himself through Christ. And God has given us this task of reconciling people to him. ¹⁹For God was in Christ, reconciling the world to himself, no longer counting people's sins against them. And he gave us this wonderful message of reconciliation. ²⁰So we are Christ's ambassadors; God is making his appeal through us. We speak for Christ when we plead, "Come back to God!" ²¹For God made Christ, who never sinned, to be the offering for our sin,* so that we could be made right with God through Christ.

6 As God's partners,* we beg you not to accept this marvelous gift of God's kindness and then ignore it. ²For God says,

5:12 Some manuscripts read *proud of yourselves.*   5:14a Or *urges us on.*   5:14b Greek *Since one died for all, then all died.*   5:21 Or *to become sin itself.*   6:1 Or *As we work together.*

He will reward us for how we have lived. God's gracious gift of salvation does not free us from the requirement of faithful obedience. All Christians must give account on the day of judgment of how they have lived (see Matthew 16:27; Romans 14:10-12; 1 Corinthians 3:10-15).

5:11 Having a "fearful responsibility to the Lord" does not mean that believers become paralyzed. On the contrary, knowing God's perfection and that he will judge everyone's actions (5:10) should spur Christians to good deeds, to what pleases our God. The fear of the Lord also frees believers from all of life's anxieties and worries. Knowing that God is "for us" (Romans 8:31) can keep believers unafraid of earthly powers—people, governments, or the forces of nature (Proverbs 3:25, 26). God takes care of his own. The fear of God gives us uncommon courage in the face of life's troubles.

5:12 Those who "brag about having a spectacular ministry rather than having a sincere heart" are the false preachers (see 2:17), who were concerned only about getting ahead in this world. They were preaching the Good News for money and popularity, while Paul and his companions were preaching out of concern for eternity. You can identify false preachers by finding out what really motivates them. If they are more concerned about themselves than about Christ, avoid them and their message.

5:13-15 Everything that Paul and his companions did was to honor God. Not only did fear of God motivate them (5:11), but Christ's love controlled their actions. The word for "controls" means "to hold fast." In other words, the love of Christ was constraining them to certain courses of action. They knew that Jesus, out of his great love, had given up his life for their sakes. He had not acted out of his own self-interest, selfishly holding on to the glory of heaven that he had already possessed (Philippians 2:6). Instead, Jesus had willingly "died for everyone." Because Christ died for us, we also are dead to our old life. Like Paul, we should no longer live to please ourselves; we should spend our life pleasing Christ.

• **5:17** Christians are brand-new people on the *inside.* The Holy Spirit gives them new life, and they are not the same anymore. We are not reformed, rehabilitated, or reeducated—we are re-created (new creations), living in vital union with Christ (Colossians 2:6, 7).

At conversion we do not merely turn over a new leaf; we begin a new life under a new Master.

While this newness is true individually, Paul is saying much more. Not only are believers changed from within, but a whole new order of creative energy began with Christ. There is a new covenant, a new perspective, a new body, a new church. All of creation is being renewed. So take notice. This is not a superficial change that will be quickly superseded by another novelty. This is an entirely new order of all creation under Christ's authority. It requires a new way of looking at all people and all of creation. Does your life reflect this new perspective?

• **5:18, 19** God brings us back to himself (reconciles us) by blotting out our sins (see also Ephesians 2:13-18) and making us right with him. When we trust in Christ, we are no longer God's enemies, or strangers or foreigners to him. Because we have been reconciled to God, we have the privilege of encouraging others to do the same, and thus we are those who have the "task of reconciling people to him."

• **5:20** An ambassador is an official representative of one country to another. As believers, we are Christ's ambassadors, sent with his message of reconciliation to the world. An ambassador of reconciliation has an important responsibility. We dare not take this responsibility lightly. How well are you fulfilling your commission as Christ's ambassador?

• **5:21** When we trust in Christ, we make an exchange: He takes our sin and makes us right with God. Our sin was laid on Christ at his crucifixion. His righteousness is given to us at our conversion. This is what Christians mean by Christ's atonement for sin. In the world, bartering works only when two people exchange goods of relatively equal value. But God offers to trade his righteousness for our sin—something of immeasurable worth for something completely worthless. How grateful we should be for his kindness to us.

6:1 How could the Corinthian believers ignore God's message? Perhaps they were doubting Paul and his words, confused by the false teachers, who taught a different message. The people heard God's message but did not let it affect what they said and did. How often do you ignore God's message?

6:2 God offers salvation to all people. Many people put off a

"At just the right time, I heard you.
    On the day of salvation, I helped you."*

Indeed, the "right time" is now. Today is the day of salvation.

Paul's Hardships

3 We live in such a way that no one will stumble because of us, and no one will find fault with our ministry. 4 In everything we do, we show that we are true ministers of God. We patiently endure troubles and hardships and calamities of every kind. 5 We have been beaten, been put in prison, faced angry mobs, worked to exhaustion, endured sleepless nights, and gone without food. 6 We prove ourselves by our purity, our understanding, our patience, our kindness, by the Holy Spirit within us,* and by our sincere love. 7 We faithfully preach the truth. God's power is working in us. We use the weapons of righteousness in the right hand for attack and the left hand for defense. 8 We serve God whether people honor us or despise us, whether they slander us or praise us. We are honest, but they call us impostors. 9 We are ignored, even though we are well known. We live close to death, but we are still alive. We have been beaten, but we have not been killed. 10 Our hearts ache, but we always have joy. We are poor, but we give spiritual riches to others. We own nothing, and yet we have everything.

11 Oh, dear Corinthian friends! We have spoken honestly with you, and our hearts are open to you. 12 There is no lack of love on our part, but you have withheld your love from us. 13 I am asking you to respond as if you were my own children. Open your hearts to us!

The Temple of the Living God

14 Don't team up with those who are unbelievers. How can righteousness be a partner with wickedness? How can light live with darkness? 15 What harmony can there be between Christ and the devil*? How can a believer be a partner with an unbeliever? 16 And what union can there be between God's temple and idols? For we are the temple of the living God. As God said:

6:3 1 Cor 8:9; 9:12
6:4 2 Cor 4:2
6:5 2 Cor 11:23-27
6:6 1 Tim 4:12
6:7 1 Cor 2:4; 2 Cor 10:4
6:8 Matt 27:63; 1 Cor 4:10, 13
6:9 Ps 118:18; 2 Cor 1:8-10; 4:10-11
6:10 Acts 3:6; Rom 8:32; 1 Cor 3:21; 2 Cor 8:9
6:11 2 Cor 7:3
6:14 Eph 5:7, 11; 1 Jn 1:6
6:16 †Lev 26:12; †Jer 32:38; Ezek 37:27

6:2 Isa 49:8 (Greek version). **6:6** Or *by our holiness of spirit*. **6:15** Greek *Beliar;* various other manuscripts render this proper name of the devil as *Belian, Beliab,* or *Belial.*

---

decision for Christ, thinking that there will be a better time—but they could easily miss their opportunity altogether. There is no time like the present to receive God's forgiveness. Don't let anything hold you back from coming to Christ. The right time is now!

6:3 In everything he did, Paul always considered what his actions communicated about Jesus Christ. If you are a believer, you are a minister for God. In the course of each day, unbelievers observe you. Don't let your careless or undisciplined actions be some person's excuse for rejecting Christ.

6:5 Being put in jail would cause many people to become bitter or to give up, but Paul saw jail time as one more opportunity to spread the Good News of Christ. Paul realized that his current circumstances weren't as important as what he did with them. Turning a bad situation into a good one, he reached out to the Roman soldiers who made up the palace guard and encouraged Christians who were afraid of persecution. We may not be in prison, but we still have plenty of opportunities to be discouraged—times of indecision, financial burdens, family conflict, church conflict, or the loss of our jobs. How we act in such situations will reflect what we believe. Like Paul, look for ways to demonstrate your faith even in bad situations. Whether or not the situation improves, your faith will grow stronger.

6:8-10 What a difference it makes to know Jesus! He cares for us in spite of what the world thinks. Christians don't have to give in to public opinion and pressure. Paul stood faithful to God whether people praised him or slandered him. He remained joyous and content in the most difficult hardships. Don't let circumstances or people's expectations control you. Be firm as you stand true to God, and refuse to compromise his standards for living.

6:11-13 "Our hearts are open to you" means that Paul had told the Corinthian believers his true feelings for them, clearly revealing how much he loved them. The Corinthians were reacting coldly to Paul's words, but Paul explained that his harsh words came from his love for them. It is easy to react against those whom God has placed over us in leadership, rather than to accept their exhortations as a sign of their love for us. We need an open rather than a closed heart toward God's messengers.

• **6:14-18** Paul urges believers to not "team up," that is, form partnerships with unbelievers because this might weaken their Christian commitment, integrity, or standards. It would be a mismatch. Earlier, Paul had explained that this did not mean isolating oneself from unbelievers (see 1 Corinthians 5:9, 10). Paul even urges Christians to stay with their unbelieving spouses (1 Corinthians 7:12, 13). He wanted believers to be active in their witness for Christ to unbelievers but not lock themselves into personal or business relationships that could cause them to compromise their faith. Believers should do everything in their power to avoid situations that could force them to divide their loyalties.

These verses also have strong application to marriage. Paul did not want single believers to enter into marriage with unbelievers. Such marriages cannot have unity in the most important issue in life—commitment and obedience to God. Because marriage involves two people becoming one, faith may become an issue, and one spouse may have to compromise beliefs for the sake of unity. Many people discount this problem only to regret it later. Don't allow emotion or passion to bind you with someone who will not be your spiritual partner. For those who have discovered God's light, there can be no fellowship or compromise with darkness (1 Corinthians 10:20, 21).

6:16 Quoting from the prophet Isaiah, Paul asserted that the church is the temple of the living God. Corinth had an abundance of temples of pagan deities, so the recipients of his letter were able to visualize the contrast the apostle intended. Those who follow Christ are not known by a building; they are known as those in whom the Spirit of God lives. The church is not where believers go, it is who they are. God is not waiting for his people in some stained-glass setting. He is always with them. That is a sobering and yet a comforting thought. How does your behavior reflect on the God you represent?

"I will live in them
and walk among them.
I will be their God,
and they will be my people.*

6:17
†Isa 52:11
Ezek 20:34

17 Therefore, come out from among unbelievers,
and separate yourselves from them, says the Lord.
Don't touch their filthy things,
and I will welcome you.*

6:18
†2 Sam 7:8, 14
Isa 43:6
Jer 31:9

18 And I will be your Father,
and you will be my sons and daughters,
says the Lord Almighty.*"

7:1
1 Pet 1:15-16

7 Because we have these promises, dear friends, let us cleanse ourselves from everything that can defile our body or spirit. And let us work toward complete holiness because we fear God.

7:2
2 Cor 6:12-13

7:3
2 Cor 6:11-12
Phil 1:7

7:4
2 Cor 8:24

2Please open your hearts to us. We have not done wrong to anyone, nor led anyone astray, nor taken advantage of anyone. 3I'm not saying this to condemn you. I said before that you are in our hearts, and we live or die together with you. 4I have the highest confidence in you, and I take great pride in you. You have greatly encouraged me and made me happy despite all our troubles.

Paul's Joy at the Church's Repentance

7:5
2 Cor 2:13; 4:8

7:6
Isa 49:13
2 Cor 1:3-4; 2:13

5When we arrived in Macedonia, there was no rest for us. We faced conflict from every direction, with battles on the outside and fear on the inside. 6But God, who encourages those who are discouraged, encouraged us by the arrival of Titus. 7His presence was a joy, but so was the news he brought of the encouragement he received from you. When he told us how much you long to see me, and how sorry you are for what happened, and how loyal you are to me, I was filled with joy!

7:8
2 Cor 2:2-4

8I am not sorry that I sent that severe letter to you, though I was sorry at first, for I know it was painful to you for a little while. 9Now I am glad I sent it, not because it hurt you, but because the pain caused you to repent and change your ways. It was the kind of sorrow God wants his people to have, so you were not harmed by us in any way. 10For the kind of sorrow God wants us to experience leads us away from sin and results in salvation. There's no regret for that kind of sorrow. But worldly sorrow, which lacks repentance, results in spiritual death.

7:10
Matt 27:3-5

6:16 Lev 26:12; Ezek 37:27.   **6:17** Isa 52:11; Ezek 20:34 (Greek version).   **6:18** 2 Sam 7:14.

• **6:17** Separation from the world involves more than keeping our distance from sinful practices; it means staying close to God. It involves more than avoiding worldly entertainment; it extends to how we spend our time and money. There is no way to separate ourselves totally from all sinful influences. Nevertheless, we are to resist the sin around us, without either giving up or giving in. When you know what God wants you to do, make a clean break with sinful practices.

7:1 Cleansing is a twofold action: turning *away* from sin, and turning *toward* God. The Corinthians were to have nothing to do with paganism. They were to make a clean break with their past and give themselves to God alone. "Work toward complete holiness" literally means "perfecting holiness." It connotes becoming mature or complete. Thus, Paul wasn't suggesting that the Corinthians could become sinless in this life. Instead, he was prodding them to work at maturing in their faith. God had provided them with all the resources they needed, and Christ's Spirit would empower them to become Christlike (Romans 8:2).

7:2 Paul insisted that the Corinthians should open their hearts for him. He knew how much those in the church need one another. If fellowship was necessary in Paul's day, it is all the more crucial today, when time is more valuable than money. Each day holds barely enough time to care for personal and family needs, let alone to meet the needs of others. Yet the activities that occupy our time are not as important as the community described in these verses. Paul's intention is not "coffee and donuts between church" fellow-

ship. Believers need accountability that comes from lives intertwined by the cords of commitment and love. If you are not in a small group Bible study, take the first steps. Offer hospitality to fellow believers; when others extend the hand of fellowship to you, grasp it enthusiastically.

7:5 Here Paul resumed the story that he left in 2:13, where he said he went to Macedonia to look for Titus. Though Paul still had many problems and hardships to face, he still found comfort and joy in the progress of the ministry.

7:8ff "That severe letter" refers to the third letter (now lost) that Paul had written to the Corinthians. Apparently it had caused the people to begin to change. For an explanation of the chronology of Paul's letters to Corinth, see the first note on 1:1.

• **7:10** Sorrow for our sins can result in changed behavior. Many people are sorry only for the effects of their sins or for being caught (sorrow "which lacks repentance"). Compare Peter's remorse and repentance with Judas's bitterness and act of suicide. Both denied Christ. One repented and was restored to faith and service; the other took his own life.

¹¹Just see what this godly sorrow produced in you! Such earnestness, such concern to clear yourselves, such indignation, such alarm, such longing to see me, such zeal, and such a readiness to punish wrong. You showed that you have done everything necessary to make things right. ¹²My purpose, then, was not to write about who did the wrong or who was wronged. I wrote to you so that in the sight of God you could see for yourselves how loyal you are to us. ¹³We have been greatly encouraged by this.

In addition to our own encouragement, we were especially delighted to see how happy Titus was about the way all of you welcomed him and set his mind* at ease. ¹⁴I had told him how proud I was of you—and you didn't disappoint me. I have always told you the truth, and now my boasting to Titus has also proved true! ¹⁵Now he cares for you more than ever when he remembers the way all of you obeyed him and welcomed him with such fear and deep respect. ¹⁶I am very happy now because I have complete confidence in you.

3. Paul defends the collection
A Call to Generous Giving

8 Now I want you to know, dear brothers and sisters,* what God in his kindness has done through the churches in Macedonia. ²They are being tested by many troubles, and they are very poor. But they are also filled with abundant joy, which has overflowed in rich generosity.

³For I can testify that they gave not only what they could afford, but far more. And they did it of their own free will. ⁴They begged us again and again for the privilege of sharing in the gift for the believers* in Jerusalem. ⁵They even did more than we had hoped, for their first action was to give themselves to the Lord and to us, just as God wanted them to do.

⁶So we have urged Titus, who encouraged your giving in the first place, to return to you and encourage you to finish this ministry of giving. ⁷Since you excel in so many ways—in your faith, your gifted speakers, your knowledge, your enthusiasm, and your love from us*— I want you to excel also in this gracious act of giving.

⁸I am not commanding you to do this. But I am testing how genuine your love is by comparing it with the eagerness of the other churches.

⁹You know the generous grace of our Lord Jesus Christ. Though he was rich, yet for your sakes he became poor, so that by his poverty he could make you rich.

7:12
1 Cor 5:1-2
2 Cor 2:3, 9

7:13
2 Cor 2:13

7:15
Phil 2:12

7:16
2 Cor 2:3
2 Thes 3:4
Phlm 1:21

8:1
Acts 16:9

8:2
2 Cor 9:11

8:4
Acts 24:17
Rom 15:26
1 Cor 16:1, 3

8:6
2 Cor 12:13, 18

8:7
1 Cor 1:5; 16:1-2
2 Cor 9:8

8:9
Matt 8:20
Phil 2:6-7

7:13 Greek *his spirit.*   **8:1** Greek *brothers.*   **8:4** Greek *for God's holy people.*   **8:7** Some manuscripts read *your love for us.*

• **7:11** Paul affirmed the Corinthians for their right response to the correction he had given them. It's difficult to accept criticism, correction, or rebuke with poise and grace. It is much more natural to be defensive and then counterattack. We can accept criticism with self-pity, thinking we don't really deserve it. We can be angry and resentful. But a mature Christian should graciously accept constructive criticism, sincerely evaluate it, and grow from it.

8:1ff Paul, writing from Macedonia, hoped that news of the generosity of these churches would encourage the Corinthian believers and motivate them to solve their problems and unite in fellowship.

• **8:2-5** During his third missionary journey, Paul had collected money for the impoverished believers in Jerusalem. The churches in Macedonia—Philippi, Thessalonica, and Berea— had given money even though they were poor, and they had sacrificially given more than Paul expected. Although they were poor themselves, they wanted to help. The amount we give is not as important as why and how we give. God does not want us to give grudgingly. Instead, he wants us to give as these churches did—out of dedication to Christ, love for fellow believers, the joy of helping those in need, as well as the fact that it was simply the good and right thing to do. How well does your giving measure up to the standards set by the Macedonian churches?

8:3-6 The Kingdom of God spreads through believers' concern and eagerness to help others. Here we see several churches joining to help others beyond their own circle of friends and their own city. Explore ways that you might link up with a ministry outside your city, either through your church or through a Christian organization. By joining with other believers to do God's work, you increase Christian unity and help the Kingdom grow.

• **8:7, 8** The Corinthian believers excelled in everything—they had faith, gifted speakers, knowledge, enthusiasm, and love. Paul encouraged them to also excel in the grace of giving. Too often, stewardship of money is given a different status than other aspects of discipleship. Most believers would not want growth in faith, knowledge, or love to stop at a certain level. Yet many decide a fixed percentage of their money to give and stay there for life. True discipleship includes growing in the mature use of all resources, so giving should expand as well. God can give you the desire and enable you to increase your capacity to give. Don't miss this opportunity for growth.

8:9 There is no evidence that Jesus was any poorer than most first-century Palestinians; rather, Jesus became poor by giving up his rights as God and becoming human. In his incarnation, God voluntarily became man—the person Jesus of Nazareth. As a man, Jesus was subject to place, time, and other human limitations. He did not give up his eternal power when he became human, but he did set aside his glory and his rights (see the note on Philippians 2:5-7). In response to the Father's will, he limited his power and knowledge. Christ became "poor" when he became human because he set aside so much. Yet by doing so, he made us "rich" because we received salvation and eternal life.

What made Jesus' humanity unique was his freedom from sin. In Jesus we can see every attribute of God's character. The Incarnation is explained further in these Bible passages: John 1:1-14; Romans 1:2-5; Philippians 2:6-11; 1 Timothy 3:16; Hebrews 2:14; 1 John 1:1-3.

8:10
2 Cor 9:2

8:12
Prov 3:27-28
Mark 12:43-44
2 Cor 9:7

8:14
Acts 4:34
2 Cor 9:12

8:15
†Exod 16:18

8:16
2 Cor 2:14

8:18
2 Cor 12:18

8:19
Acts 14:23
1 Cor 16:3-4

8:21
Prov 3:4
Rom 12:17

¹⁰Here is my advice: It would be good for you to finish what you started a year ago. Last year you were the first who wanted to give, and you were the first to begin doing it. ¹¹Now you should finish what you started. Let the eagerness you showed in the beginning be matched now by your giving. Give in proportion to what you have. ¹²Whatever you give is acceptable if you give it eagerly. And give according to what you have, not what you don't have. ¹³Of course, I don't mean your giving should make life easy for others and hard for yourselves. I only mean that there should be some equality. ¹⁴Right now you have plenty and can help those who are in need. Later, they will have plenty and can share with you when you need it. In this way, things will be equal. ¹⁵As the Scriptures say,

"Those who gathered a lot had nothing left over,
    and those who gathered only a little had enough."*

Titus and His Companions

¹⁶But thank God! He has given Titus the same enthusiasm for you that I have. ¹⁷Titus welcomed our request that he visit you again. In fact, he himself was very eager to go and see you. ¹⁸We are also sending another brother with Titus. All the churches praise him as a preacher of the Good News. ¹⁹He was appointed by the churches to accompany us as we take the offering to Jerusalem*—a service that glorifies the Lord and shows our eagerness to help.

²⁰We are traveling together to guard against any criticism for the way we are handling this generous gift. ²¹We are careful to be honorable before the Lord, but we also want everyone else to see that we are honorable.

²²We are also sending with them another of our brothers who has proven himself many

8:15 Exod 16:18.   **8:19** See 1 Cor 16:3-4.

PRINCIPLES OF CONFRONTATION IN 2 CORINTHIANS	Method	Reference
	Be firm and bold	7:9; 10:2
	Affirm all you see that is good	7:4
	Be accurate and honest	7:14; 8:21
	Know the facts	11:22-27
	Follow up after the confrontation	7:13; 12:14
	Be gentle after being firm	7:15; 13:11-13
	Speak words that reflect Christ's message, not your own ideas	10:3; 10:12, 13; 12:19
	Use discipline only when all else fails.	13:2

Sometimes rebuke is necessary, but it must be used with caution. The purpose of any rebuke, confrontation, or discipline is to help people, not hurt them.

• **8:10-15** The Christians in the Corinthian church had money, and apparently they had planned to collect money for the Jerusalem church a year previously (see also 9:2). Paul challenges them to act on their plans. Four principles of giving emerge here: (1) Your willingness to give enthusiastically is more important than the amount you give; (2) you should strive to fulfill your financial commitments; (3) if you give to others in need, they will, in turn, help you when you are in need; (4) you should give as a response to Christ, not for anything you can get out of it. How you give reflects your devotion to Christ.

• **8:12** How do you decide how much to give? What about differences in the financial resources Christians have? Paul gives the Corinthian church several principles to follow: (1) Each person should follow through on previous promises (8:10, 11; 9:3); (2) each person should give as much as he or she is able (8:12; 9:6); (3) each person must make up his or her own mind how much to give (9:7); and (4) each person should give in proportion to what God has given him or her (9:10). God gives to us so that we can give to others.

• **8:12** Paul says that we should give of what we have, not what we don't have. Sacrificial giving must be responsible. Paul wants believers to give generously, but not to the extent that those who

depend on the givers (their families, for example) must go without having their basic needs met. Give until it hurts, but don't give so that it hurts your family and/or relatives who need your financial support.

8:18-21 "Another brother" was traveling with Paul and Titus, a man who was elected by the churches to also take the large financial gift to Jerusalem. Paul explained that by traveling together there could be no suspicion and people would know that the gift was being handled honestly. The church did not need to worry that the bearers of the collection would misuse the money.

Paul used every safeguard to maintain integrity in the collection of money for the Jerusalem church. Those outside the church can view skeptically the way believers handle money in the church. Financial scandals among high-profile ministries have alerted the non-believing world to the unethical gimmicks that some Christians use. It is possible to avoid mismanagement of God's resources. Does your church or organization have a system of checks and balances that prevent wrongful behavior? Are there financial practices in your ministry that need to be reviewed? Christians must have the highest standard of financial responsibility.

times and has shown on many occasions how eager he is. He is now even more enthusiastic because of his great confidence in you. 23If anyone asks about Titus, say that he is my partner who works with me to help you. And the brothers with him have been sent by the churches,* and they bring honor to Christ. 24So show them your love, and prove to all the churches that our boasting about you is justified.

8:23
Phil 2:25
8:24
2 Cor 7:4

The Collection for Christians in Jerusalem

9 I really don't need to write to you about this ministry of giving for the believers in Jerusalem.* 2For I know how eager you are to help, and I have been boasting to the churches in Macedonia that you in Greece* were ready to send an offering a year ago. In fact, it was your enthusiasm that stirred up many of the Macedonian believers to begin giving.

9:1
Acts 24:17
2 Cor 8:4, 20
9:2
2 Cor 8:11-12, 19

3But I am sending these brothers to be sure you really are ready, as I have been telling them, and that your money is all collected. I don't want to be wrong in my boasting about you. 4We would be embarrassed—not to mention your own embarrassment—if some Macedonian believers came with me and found that you weren't ready after all I had told them! 5So I thought I should send these brothers ahead of me to make sure the gift you promised is ready. But I want it to be a willing gift, not one given grudgingly.

9:3
1 Cor 16:2
2 Cor 8:23

9:5
Phil 4:17

6Remember this—a farmer who plants only a few seeds will get a small crop. But the one who plants generously will get a generous crop. 7You must each decide in your heart how much to give. And don't give reluctantly or in response to pressure. "For God loves a person who gives cheerfully."* 8And God will generously provide all you need. Then you will always have everything you need and plenty left over to share with others. 9As the Scriptures say,

9:6
Prov 11:24-25; 22:9
Gal 6:7, 9
9:7
Exod 25:2
Deut 15:7-10
2 Cor 8:12
9:8
Phil 4:19
9:9
†Ps 112:9

"They share freely and give generously to the poor.
    Their good deeds will be remembered forever."*

10For God is the one who provides seed for the farmer and then bread to eat. In the same way, he will provide and increase your resources and then produce a great harvest of generosity* in you.

9:10
Isa 55:10
Hos 10:12

11Yes, you will be enriched in every way so that you can always be generous. And when we take your gifts to those who need them, they will thank God. 12So two good things will result from this ministry of giving—the needs of the believers in Jerusalem* will be met, and they will joyfully express their thanks to God.

9:11
2 Cor 1:11; 4:15
9:12
2 Cor 8:14

13As a result of your ministry, they will give glory to God. For your generosity to them and to all believers will prove that you are obedient to the Good News of Christ. 14And they will pray for you with deep affection because of the overflowing grace God has given to you. 15Thank God for this gift* too wonderful for words!

8:23 Greek *are apostles of the churches.* **9:1** Greek *about the offering for God's holy people.* **9:2** Greek *in Achaia, the southern region of the Greek peninsula. Macedonia was in the northern region of Greece.* **9:7** See footnote on Prov 22:8. **9:9** Ps 112:9. **9:10** Greek *righteousness.* **9:12** Greek *of God's holy people.* **9:15** Greek *his gift.*

9:1, 2 By describing how their own "enthusiasm" had incited the Macedonians to give, Paul was, in effect, prodding the Corinthians to rekindle their initial enthusiasm for giving. Paul wasn't naive about human behavior. The start and end of a marathon are much more thrilling than the miles in between. It takes stubborn determination to keep going. Paul also knew that it took a community to persevere. Just as teammates will cheer their runner on in a race, so Paul was sending Titus and two other believers to the Corinthians to cheer them on.

• **9:3-5** Paul reminded the Corinthians to fulfill the commitment that they had already made (see also 8:10-12). They had said that they would collect a financial gift to send to the church in Jerusalem. Paul was sending a few men ahead of him to make sure their gift was ready, so it would be a real gift and not look like people had to give under pressure at the last minute. He was holding them accountable to keep their promise, so that neither Paul nor the Corinthians would be embarrassed.

• **9:6-8** People may hesitate to give generously to God because they worry about having enough money left over to meet their own needs. Paul assured the Corinthians that God was able to meet their needs. The person who gives only a little will receive

only a little in return. Don't let a lack of faith keep you from giving cheerfully and generously.

• **9:7** A giving attitude is more important than the amount given. The person who can give only a small gift shouldn't be embarrassed. God is concerned about *how* a person gives from his or her resources (see Mark 12:41-44). According to that standard, the giving of the Macedonian churches would be difficult to match (8:3). God himself is a cheerful giver. Consider all he has done for us. He is pleased when we who are created in his image give generously and joyfully. Do you have a difficult time letting go of your money? It may reflect ungratefulness to God.

• **9:10** God gives us resources to use and invest for him. Paul uses the illustration of seed to explain that the resources God gives us are not to be hidden, foolishly devoured, or thrown away. Instead, they should be cultivated in order to produce more crops. When we invest what God has given us in his work, he will provide us with even more to give in his service.

• **9:13** Paul wanted his readers to be generous on every occasion. As he appealed to the Corinthians to give sacrificially to aid the Jerusalem congregation, he reminded them that God is the source of everything good (9:10). Believers are called to be generous because of the example of the Lord of life. A stingy Christian

4. Paul defends his authority

10:1
1 Cor 2:3
2 Cor 10:10

10:2
1 Cor 4:21

10:4
Jer 1:10
Eph 6:13-17

10:5
Isa 2:11-12
1 Cor 1:19

10:6
2 Cor 2:9; 7:15

10:7
John 7:24
2 Cor 11:23

10:8
2 Cor 12:6; 13:10

10:10
1 Cor 1:17; 2:3
2 Cor 11:6
Gal 4:13-14

10:11
2 Cor 13:2, 10

10:12
2 Cor 3:1; 5:12

10 Now I, Paul, appeal to you with the gentleness and kindness of Christ—though I realize you think I am timid in person and bold only when I write from far away. ²Well, I am begging you now so that when I come I won't have to be bold with those who think we act from human motives.

³We are human, but we don't wage war as humans do. ⁴*We use God's mighty weapons, not worldly weapons, to knock down the strongholds of human reasoning and to destroy false arguments. ⁵We destroy every proud obstacle that keeps people from knowing God. We capture their rebellious thoughts and teach them to obey Christ. ⁶And after you have become fully obedient, we will punish everyone who remains disobedient.

⁷Look at the obvious facts.* Those who say they belong to Christ must recognize that we belong to Christ as much as they do. ⁸I may seem to be boasting too much about the authority given to us by the Lord. But our authority builds you up; it doesn't tear you down. So I will not be ashamed of using my authority.

⁹I'm not trying to frighten you by my letters. ¹⁰For some say, "Paul's letters are demanding and forceful, but in person he is weak, and his speeches are worthless!" ¹¹Those people should realize that our actions when we arrive in person will be as forceful as what we say in our letters from far away.

¹²Oh, don't worry; we wouldn't dare say that we are as wonderful as these other men who tell you how important they are! But they are only comparing themselves with each other, using themselves as the standard of measurement. How ignorant!

10:4 English translations divide verses 4 and 5 in various ways. **10:7** Or *You look at things only on the basis of appearance.*

RAISING FUNDS HONORABLY

Be dedicated to God 8:5	Be accountable 9:3
Provide information 8:4	Let people give willingly 9:7
Show definite purpose and goal . . 8:4	Be generous yourselves. 8:7
Be enthusiastic 8:7, 8, 11	Have someone to keep it moving 8:18-22
Reveal honesty and integrity 8:21	Be persistent, trusting God to provide. . 8:2ff

The topic of fund-raising is not one to be avoided or one that should embarrass us, but all fund-raising efforts should be planned and conducted responsibly.

---

should be an extinct species. Generosity proves that a person's heart has been cleansed of self-interest and filled with the servant spirit of Jesus himself. That is why acts of generosity result in God being praised. Do neighbors see generosity in your actions?

10:1, 2 Paul's opponents questioned his authority. From 7:8-16 we know that the majority of Corinthian believers sided with Paul. However, a minority continued to slander him, saying that he was bold in his letters but had no authority in person. Chapters 10–13 are Paul's response to this charge.

10:3-6 We, like Paul, are merely weak humans, but we don't need to use human plans and methods to win our battles. God's mighty weapons are available to us as we fight against the devil's "strongholds." The Christian must choose whose methods to use—God's or the world's. Paul assures us that God's mighty weapons—prayer, faith, hope, love, God's Word, the Holy Spirit—are powerful and effective (see Ephesians 6:13-18)! These weapons can break down the proud human arguments against God and the walls that Satan builds to keep people from finding God. When dealing with people's proud arguments that keep them from a relationship with Christ, we may be tempted to use our own methods. But nothing can break down these barriers like God's weapons.

10:5 Paul uses military terminology to describe this warfare against sin and Satan. God must be the commander in chief— even our thoughts must be submitted to his control as we live for him. Spirit-empowered believers must capture every thought and yield it to Christ. When exposed to ideas or opportunities that might lead to wrong desires, you have a choice. You can recognize the danger and turn away, or you can allow unhealthy thoughts to take you captive. You capture your fantasies and

desires when you honestly admit them to the Lord and ask him to redirect your thinking. Ask God to give you the spirit of discernment to keep your thoughts focused on his truth.

10:7-10 Those who opposed Paul portrayed him as weak and powerless, but Paul reminded the Corinthians that he had been given authority by the Lord. False teachers were encouraging the believers to ignore Paul, but Paul explained that the advice in his letters was to be taken seriously. He had authority because he and his companions had been the first to bring the Good News to Corinth (10:14). Everyone knew that because of this service, their faith had been built up.

10:10 Some said that Paul's speaking amounted to nothing. Greece was known for its eloquent and persuasive orators. Evidently, some were judging Paul by comparing him to other speakers they had heard, and Paul was perhaps not the most powerful preacher (although he was an excellent debater). But Paul responded obediently to God's call and thus introduced Christianity to the Roman Empire. Moses and Jeremiah also had problems with speaking (see Exodus 4:10-12; Jeremiah 1:6). Preaching ability is not the first prerequisite of a great leader!

● **10:12, 13** Paul criticized the false teachers who were trying to prove their goodness by comparing themselves with others rather than with God's standards. When we compare ourselves with others, we may feel proud because we think we're better. But when we measure ourselves against God's standards, it becomes obvious that we have no basis for pride. Don't worry about other people's accomplishments. Instead, ask yourself: How does my life measure up to what God wants? How does my life compare to that of Jesus Christ?

13 We will not boast about things done outside our area of authority. We will boast only about what has happened within the boundaries of the work God has given us, which includes our working with you. 14 We are not reaching beyond these boundaries when we claim authority over you, as if we had never visited you. For we were the first to travel all the way to Corinth with the Good News of Christ.

10:13
Rom 12:3

10:14
1 Cor 9:1

15 Nor do we boast and claim credit for the work someone else has done. Instead, we hope that your faith will grow so that the boundaries of our work among you will be extended. 16 Then we will be able to go and preach the Good News in other places far beyond you, where no one else is working. Then there will be no question of our boasting about work done in someone else's territory. 17 As the Scriptures say, "If you want to boast, boast only about the LORD."*

10:15
Rom 15:20
2 Thes 1:3

10:16
Acts 19:21

10:17
†Jer 9:24
1 Cor 1:31

18 When people commend themselves, it doesn't count for much. The important thing is for the Lord to commend them.

10:18
Prov 27:2

Paul and the False Apostles

11 I hope you will put up with a little more of my foolishness. Please bear with me. 2 For I am jealous for you with the jealousy of God himself. I promised you as a pure bride* to one husband—Christ. 3 But I fear that somehow your pure and undivided devotion to Christ will be corrupted, just as Eve was deceived by the cunning ways of the serpent. 4 You happily put up with whatever anyone tells you, even if they preach a different Jesus than the one we preach, or a different kind of Spirit than the one you received, or a different kind of gospel than the one you believed.

11:2
Hos 2:19
Eph 5:26-27

11:3
Gen 3:1-6, 13
John 8:44
1 Tim 2:14

11:4
Rom 8:15
Gal 1:6-8

5 But I don't consider myself inferior in any way to these "super apostles" who teach such things. 6 I may be unskilled as a speaker, but I'm not lacking in knowledge. We have made this clear to you in every possible way.

11:5
Gal 2:6

11:6
1 Cor 1:17
Eph 3:4

7 Was I wrong when I humbled myself and honored you by preaching God's Good News to you without expecting anything in return? 8 I "robbed" other churches by accepting their contributions so I could serve you at no cost. 9 And when I was with you and didn't have enough to live on, I did not become a financial burden to anyone. For the brothers who came

11:7
1 Cor 9:12, 18
2 Cor 12:13

11:9
2 Cor 12:13

10:17 Jer 9:24. **11:2** Greek *a virgin.*

• **10:17, 18** When we do something well, we want to tell others and be recognized. But recognition is dangerous—it can lead to inflated pride. How much better it is to seek the praise of God rather than the praise of people. Then, when we receive praise, we will be free to give God the credit. What should you change about the way you live in order to receive God's commendation?

• **11:1** Paul asked the Corinthian believers to bear with him as he talked more "foolishness." In other words, Paul felt foolish rehearsing his credentials as a preacher of the Good News (11:16-21). But he thought that he had to do this in order to silence the false teachers (11:13).

11:2 Paul was anxious that the church's love should be for Christ alone, just as a pure bride saves her love for one man only. By "pure bride" he meant one who was unaffected by false doctrine.

• **11:3** The Corinthians' pure and simple devotion to Christ was being threatened by false teaching. Paul did not want the believers to lose their single-minded love for Christ. Keeping Christ first in your life can be very difficult when you have so many distractions threatening to sidetrack your faith. Just as Eve lost her focus by listening to the serpent, you, too, can lose your focus by letting your life become overcrowded and confused. Is there anything that weakens your commitment to keep Christ first in your life? How can you minimize the distractions that threaten your devotion to him?

• **11:4** The Corinthian believers were falling for smooth talk and messages that sounded good and seemed to make sense. Today there are many false teachings that seem to make sense. Don't believe someone simply because he or she sounds like an authority or says words you like to hear. Search the Bible and check his or her teachings against God's Word. The Bible should be your authoritative guide. The false teachers distorted the truth about Jesus and ended up preaching a different Jesus, a different spirit than the Holy Spirit, and a different way of salvation. Those who

teach anything different from what God's infallible Word says are both mistaken and misleading.

11:5 Paul was saying that these marvelous teachers ("super apostles") were no better than he was. They may have been more eloquent speakers, but they spoke lies and were servants of Satan.

• **11:6** Paul, a brilliant thinker, was not a trained, eloquent speaker. Although his ministry was effective (see Acts 17), he had not been trained in the Greek schools of oratory and speechmaking, as many of the false teachers probably had been. Paul believed in a simple presentation of the Good News (see 1 Corinthians 1:17), and some people thought this showed simple-mindedness. Thus, Paul's speaking performance was often used against him by false teachers.

Content is far more important than the presentation. A simple, clear presentation that helps listeners understand will be of great value. God's Word stands on its own merit and is not dependent on imperfect human beings to create its own hearing. Many people feel that if they can't sing, speak, teach, or preach as well as their idolized heroes, they are insecure about saying or doing anything. Don't apologize for your inadequacies. Accept your limitations with the same humility that you accept the strengths God has given you.

• **11:7** The Corinthians may have thought that preachers could be judged by how much money they demanded. A good speaker would charge a large sum, a fair speaker would be a little cheaper, and a poor speaker would speak for free. The false teachers may have argued that because Paul asked no fee for his preaching, he must have been an amateur, with little authority or competence. Believers today must be careful not to assume that every preacher or evangelist who is well known or who demands a large honorarium necessarily teaches the truth.

11:7-12 Paul could have asked the Corinthian church for financial support. Jesus himself taught that those who minister for God should be supported by the people to whom they minister (Matthew 10:10). But Paul thought that asking for support* in Corinth might

from Macedonia brought me all that I needed. I have never been a burden to you, and I never will be. 10As surely as the truth of Christ is in me, no one in all of Greece* will ever stop me from boasting about this. 11Why? Because I don't love you? God knows that I do.

12But I will continue doing what I have always done. This will undercut those who are looking for an opportunity to boast that their work is just like ours. 13These people are false apostles. They are deceitful workers who disguise themselves as apostles of Christ. 14But I

11:11
2 Cor 7:3; 12:15

11:12
1 Cor 9:12

11:13
Rev 2:2

11:10 Greek *Achaia*, the southern region of the Greek peninsula.

PAUL'S CREDENTIALS

One of Paul's biggest problems with the church in Corinth was his concern that they viewed him as no more than a blustering preacher; thus, they were not taking seriously his advice in his letters and on his visits. Paul addressed this attitude in the letter of 2 Corinthians, pointing out his credentials as an apostle of Christ and why the Corinthians should take his advice.

Reference	Credential
1:1, 21; 4:1	Commissioned by God
1:12	Acted in holiness, sincerity, and dependence on God alone in his dealings with them
1:13, 14	Was straightforward and sincere in his letters
1:18; 4:2	Spoke truthfully
1:22	Had God's Holy Spirit
2:4; 6:11; 11:11	Loved the Corinthian believers
2:17	Spoke with sincerity and Christ's authority
3:2, 3	Worked among them and changed their lives
4:1, 16	Did not give up
4:2	Taught the Bible with integrity
4:5	Had Christ as the center of his message
4:8-12; 6:4, 5, 9, 10	Endured persecution as he taught the Good News
5:18-20	Was Christ's ambassador, called to tell the Good News
6:3, 4	Tried to live an exemplary life so others would not be kept from God
6:6	Led a pure life, understood the gospel, and displayed patience with the Corinthians
6:7	Was truthful and filled with God's power
6:8	Stood true to God first and always
7:2; 11:7-9	Never led anyone astray or took advantage of anyone
8:20, 21	Handled their offering for the Jerusalem believers in a responsible, blameless manner
10:1-6	Used God's weapons, not his own, for God's work
10:7, 8	Was confident that he belonged to Christ
10:12, 13	Would boast not in himself but in the Lord
10:14, 15	Had authority because he taught them the Good News
11:23-33	Endured pain and danger as he fulfilled his calling
12:2-4	Was blessed with an astounding vision
12:6	Lived as an example to the believers
12:7-10	Was constantly humbled by a "thorn" in the flesh that God refused to take away
12:12	Did miracles among them
12:19	Was always motivated to strengthen others spiritually
13:4	Was filled with God's power
13:5, 6	Passed the test
13:9	Was always concerned that his spiritual children become mature believers

---

be misunderstood. There were many false teachers who hoped to make a good profit from preaching (2:17), and Paul might look like one of them. Paul separated himself completely from those false teachers in order to silence those who only claimed to do God's work.

• **11:14, 15** One Jewish writing (the Apocalypse of Moses) says that the story of Eve's temptation includes Satan masquerading as an angel. Paul may have been thinking of this story, or he could have been referring to Satan's typical devices. In either case, nothing could be more deceitful than Satan, the prince of darkness (Ephesians 6:12; Colossians 1:13), disguising himself as an angel of light. In the same way, these false apostles were pretending to be apostles of Christ, while in reality they were agents of Satan.

• **11:14, 15** Satan and his servants can deceive us by appearing to be attractive, good, and moral. Many unsuspecting people follow smooth-talking, Bible-quoting leaders into cults that alienate them from their families and lead them into the practice of immorality and deceit. Don't be fooled by external appearances. Our impressions alone are not an accurate indicator of who is or isn't a true follower of Christ; so it helps to ask these questions: (1) Do the teachings confirm Scripture (Acts 17:11)? (2) Does the teacher affirm and proclaim that Jesus Christ is God, who came into the world as a man to save people from their sins (1 John 4:1-3)? (3) Is the teacher's lifestyle consistent with biblical morality (Matthew 12:33-37)?

am not surprised! Even Satan disguises himself as an angel of light. 15So it is no wonder that his servants also disguise themselves as servants of righteousness. In the end they will get the punishment their wicked deeds deserve. **11:15** Phil 3:19

Paul's Many Trials

16Again I say, don't think that I am a fool to talk like this. But even if you do, listen to me, as you would to a foolish person, while I also boast a little. 17Such boasting is not from the Lord, but I am acting like a fool. 18And since others boast about their human achievements, I will, too. 19After all, you think you are so wise, but you enjoy putting up with fools! 20You put up with it when someone enslaves you, takes everything you have, takes advantage of you, takes control of everything, and slaps you in the face. 21I'm ashamed to say that we've been too "weak" to do that! **11:16** 2 Cor 12:6 **11:18** Phil 3:3-4 **11:20** Gal 2:4; 4:9 **11:21** 2 Cor 10:10

But whatever they dare to boast about—I'm talking like a fool again—I dare to boast about it, too. 22Are they Hebrews? So am I. Are they Israelites? So am I. Are they descendants of Abraham? So am I. 23Are they servants of Christ? I know I sound like a madman, but I have served him far more! I have worked harder, been put in prison more often, been whipped times without number, and faced death again and again. 24Five different times the Jewish leaders gave me thirty-nine lashes. 25Three times I was beaten with rods. Once I was stoned. Three times I was shipwrecked. Once I spent a whole night and a day adrift at sea. 26I have traveled on many long journeys. I have faced danger from rivers and from robbers. I have faced danger from my own people, the Jews, as well as from the Gentiles. I have faced danger in the cities, in the deserts, and on the seas. And I have faced danger from men who claim to be believers but are not.* 27I have worked hard and long, enduring many sleepless nights. I have been hungry and thirsty and have often gone without food. I have shivered in the cold, without enough clothing to keep me warm. **11:22** Rom 11:1 Phil 3:5 **11:23** Rom 8:36 1 Cor 15:10 2 Cor 6:4-5 **11:24** Deut 25:3 **11:25** Acts 14:19; 16:22; 27:41 **11:26** Acts 9:23; 14:5; 20:3; 21:31 Gal 2:4 **11:27** 1 Cor 4:11 2 Cor 6:5

28Then, besides all this, I have the daily burden of my concern for all the churches. 29Who is weak without my feeling that weakness? Who is led astray, and I do not burn with anger? **11:29** 1 Cor 9:22

30If I must boast, I would rather boast about the things that show how weak I am. 31God, the Father of our Lord Jesus, who is worthy of eternal praise, knows I am not lying. 32When I was in Damascus, the governor under King Aretas kept guards at the city gates to catch me. 33I had to be lowered in a basket through a window in the city wall to escape from him. **11:30** 2 Cor 12:5 **11:31** 2 Cor 1:23 **11:32-33** Acts 9:24-25

Paul's Vision and His Thorn in the Flesh

12 This boasting will do no good, but I must go on. I will reluctantly tell about visions and revelations from the Lord. 2I* was caught up to the third heaven fourteen years ago. Whether I was in my body or out of my body, I don't know—only God knows. 3Yes, only **12:1** Gal 1:12

11:26 Greek *from false brothers.* **12:2** Greek *I know a man in Christ who.*

11:15 Paul reminds the Corinthians that the false teachers and hypocritical leaders will one day "get the punishment their wicked deeds deserve." The principle of judgment applies to all who speak on God's behalf. The apostle James said that teachers will be judged by the Lord with closer scrutiny than will those who sit under their teaching (James 3:1). If it is not already your practice, each time you sit down with the Scriptures to prepare a lesson or a sermon, spend some quiet moments in prayer asking the Holy Spirit to guide your preparation.

• **11:22, 23** Paul presented his credentials to counteract the charges that the false teachers were making against him. He felt foolish boasting like this, but his list of credentials would silence any doubts about his authority. Paul wanted to keep the Corinthians from slipping under the spell of the false teachers and turning away from the Good News. Paul also gave a list of his credentials in his letter to the Philippians (see Philippians 3:4-8).

• **11:23-29** Paul was angry that the false teachers had impressed and deceived the Corinthians (11:13-15). Therefore, he had reestablished his credibility and authority by listing the trials he had endured in his service for Christ. Some of these trials are recorded in the book of Acts (Acts 14:19; 16:22-24). Because Paul wrote this letter during his third missionary journey (Acts 18:23–21:17), his trials weren't over. He would experience yet further difficulties and humiliations for the cause of Christ (see Acts 21:30-33; 22:24-30). Paul was sacrificing his life for the Good

News, something the false teachers would never do. The trials and hurts we experience for Christ's sake build our character, demonstrate our faith, and prepare us for further service to the Lord.

11:25 Sea travel was not as safe as it is today. Paul had been shipwrecked three times, and he would face another accident on his voyage to Rome (see Acts 27). By this time, Paul had probably made at least eight or nine voyages.

11:28, 29 Not only did Paul face beatings and dangers, he also carried the daily concern for the young churches, worrying that they were staying true to the Good News and free from false teachings and inner strife. Paul was concerned for individuals in the churches he served. If God has placed you in a position of leadership and authority, treat people with Paul's kind of empathy and concern.

11:32, 33 King Aretas, king of the Nabateans (Edomites) from 9 B.C. to A.D. 40, had appointed a governor to oversee the Nabatean segment of the population in Damascus. Somehow the Jews in Damascus had been able to enlist this governor to help them try to capture Paul (see Acts 9:22-25). Paul gave a "for instance" here, describing his escape from Damascus in a basket lowered from a window in the city wall. Paul recounted this incident to show what he had endured for Christ. The false teachers couldn't make such claims.

12:2, 3 Paul continued his "boasting" by telling about visions and revelations he had received from the Lord. Paul explained that

12:4
Luke 23:43
Rev 2:7

12:5
2 Cor 11:30

12:6
2 Cor 10:8

12:7
Job 2:6

12:8
Matt 26:39, 44

12:9
Phil 4:13

12:10
2 Cor 6:4; 13:4

12:11
2 Cor 11:1, 5

12:12
Rom 15:19

12:13
1 Cor 9:12, 18
2 Cor 11:7

12:14
1 Cor 4:14-15
2 Cor 13:1

12:15
2 Cor 11:11
Phil 2:17
1 Thes 2:8

12:16
2 Cor 11:9

God knows whether I was in my body or outside my body. But I do know [4] that I was caught up* to paradise and heard things so astounding that they cannot be expressed in words, things no human is allowed to tell.

[5] That experience is worth boasting about, but I'm not going to do it. I will boast only about my weaknesses. [6] If I wanted to boast, I would be no fool in doing so, because I would be telling the truth. But I won't do it, because I don't want anyone to give me credit beyond what they can see in my life or hear in my message, [7] even though I have received such wonderful revelations from God. So to keep me from becoming proud, I was given a thorn in my flesh, a messenger from Satan to torment me and keep me from becoming proud.

[8] Three different times I begged the Lord to take it away. [9] Each time he said, "My grace is all you need. My power works best in weakness." So now I am glad to boast about my weaknesses, so that the power of Christ can work through me. [10] That's why I take pleasure in my weaknesses, and in the insults, hardships, persecutions, and troubles that I suffer for Christ. For when I am weak, then I am strong.

Paul's Concern for the Corinthians

[11] You have made me act like a fool—boasting like this.* You ought to be writing commendations for me, for I am not at all inferior to these "super apostles," even though I am nothing at all. [12] When I was with you, I certainly gave you proof that I am an apostle. For I patiently did many signs and wonders and miracles among you. [13] The only thing I failed to do, which I do in the other churches, was to become a financial burden to you. Please forgive me for this wrong!

[14] Now I am coming to you for the third time, and I will not be a burden to you. I don't want what you have—I want you. After all, children don't provide for their parents. Rather, parents provide for their children. [15] I will gladly spend myself and all I have for you, even though it seems that the more I love you, the less you love me.

[16] Some of you admit I was not a burden to you. But others still think I was sneaky and

12:3-4 Greek *But I know such a man,* [4]*that he was caught up.*   **12:11** Some manuscripts do not include *boasting like this.*

---

he didn't know if he was taken up in his body or in his spirit, but he had been in paradise ("the third heaven," perhaps referring to the highest part of the heavens, beyond the atmosphere and the stars, where God himself lives). This incident cannot be positively identified with a recorded event in Paul's career, although some think this may have been when he was stoned and left for dead (Acts 14:19, 20). Paul told about this incident to show that he had been uniquely touched by God.

• **12:7, 8** We don't know what Paul's thorn in the flesh was because he doesn't tell us. Some have suggested that it was malaria, epilepsy, or a disease of the eyes (see Galatians 4:13-15). Whatever the case, it was a chronic and debilitating problem, which at times kept him from working. This thorn was a hindrance to his ministry, and he prayed for its removal; but God refused. Paul was a very self-sufficient person, so this thorn must have been difficult for him.

Three times Paul prayed for healing and did not receive it. He received, however, things far greater because he received greater grace from God, a stronger character, humility, and an ability to empathize with others. In addition, it benefited those around him as they saw God at work in his life. God, according to his sovereign plan, doesn't heal some believers of their physical ailments. We don't know why some are spared and others aren't. God chooses according to his divine purposes. Our task is to pray, to believe, and to trust. Paul is living proof that holy living and courageous faith do not ensure instant physical healing. When we pray for healing, we must trust our bodies to God's care. We must recognize that nothing separates us from his love (Romans 8:35-39) and that our spiritual condition is always more important than our physical condition.

• **12:9** Although God did not remove Paul's affliction, he promised to demonstrate his power in Paul. The fact that God's power is displayed in our weaknesses should give us courage and hope. As we recognize our limitations, we will depend more on God for our effectiveness rather than on our own energy, effort, or talent. Our limitations not only help develop Christian character but also deepen our worship, because in admitting them, we affirm God's strength.

• **12:10** When we are strong in abilities or resources, we are tempted to do God's work on our own, and that can lead to pride. When we are weak, allowing God to fill us with *his* power, then we are stronger than we could ever be on our own. God does not intend for us to be weak, passive, or ineffective—life provides enough hindrances and setbacks without us creating them. When those obstacles come, we must depend on God. Only his power will make us effective for him and will help us do work that has lasting value.

• **12:11-15** Paul was not merely revealing his feelings; he was defending his authority as an apostle of Jesus Christ. Paul was hurt that the church in Corinth doubted and questioned him, so he defended himself for the cause of the Good News, not to satisfy his ego. When you are "put on trial," do you think only about saving your reputation or are you more concerned about what people will think about Christ?

12:13 Paul explained that the only thing he did in the other churches that he didn't do in Corinth was to become a burden—to ask the believers to feed and house him. When he said, "Forgive me for this wrong," he was clearly being sarcastic. He actually did more for the Corinthians than for any other church, but still they misunderstood him.

12:14 Paul had founded the church in Corinth on his first visit there (Acts 18:1). He subsequently made a second visit (2:1). He was planning what would be his third visit (see also 13:1). Paul explained that, as before, he didn't want to be paid, fed, or housed; he only wanted the believers to be nourished with the spiritual food he would feed them.

12:16-19 Although Paul asked nothing of the Corinthian believers, some doubters were still saying that Paul must have been sneaky and made money from them somehow. But Paul again explained that everything he did for the believers was for their edification, not to enrich himself.

took advantage of you by trickery. [17]But how? Did any of the men I sent to you take advantage of you? [18]When I urged Titus to visit you and sent our other brother with him, did Titus take advantage of you? No! For we have the same spirit and walk in each other's steps, doing things the same way.

12:18
2 Cor 8:6, 16-18

[19]Perhaps you think we're saying these things just to defend ourselves. No, we tell you this as Christ's servants, and with God as our witness. Everything we do, dear friends, is to strengthen you. [20]For I am afraid that when I come I won't like what I find, and you won't like my response. I am afraid that I will find quarreling, jealousy, anger, selfishness, slander, gossip, arrogance, and disorderly behavior. [21]Yes, I am afraid that when I come again, God will humble me in your presence. And I will be grieved because many of you have not given up your old sins. You have not repented of your impurity, sexual immorality, and eagerness for lustful pleasure.

12:19
Rom 9:1

12:20
1 Cor 4:21
2 Cor 2:1-4

12:21
2 Cor 13:2

Paul's Final Advice

13 This is the third time I am coming to visit you (and as the Scriptures say, "The facts of every case must be established by the testimony of two or three witnesses"*). [2]I have already warned those who had been sinning when I was there on my second visit. Now I again warn them and all others, just as I did before, that next time I will not spare them.

13:1
†Deut 19:15
Matt 18:16
2 Cor 12:14
1 Tim 5:19

[3]I will give you all the proof you want that Christ speaks through me. Christ is not weak when he deals with you; he is powerful among you. [4]Although he was crucified in weakness, he now lives by the power of God. We, too, are weak, just as Christ was, but when we deal with you we will be alive with him and will have God's power.

13:2
2 Cor 1:23; 12:21

13:3
Matt 10:20
1 Cor 5:4

13:4
Rom 1:4; 6:4
Phil 2:7-8
1 Pet 3:18

[5]Examine yourselves to see if your faith is genuine. Test yourselves. Surely you know that Jesus Christ is among you*; if not, you have failed the test of genuine faith. [6]As you test yourselves, I hope you will recognize that we have not failed the test of apostolic authority.

13:5
John 14:20;
17:23, 26
Rom 8:10
1 Cor 11:28
Gal 4:19
Col 1:27

[7]We pray to God that you will not do what is wrong by refusing our correction. I hope we won't need to demonstrate our authority when we arrive. Do the right thing before we come—even if that makes it look like we have failed to demonstrate our authority. [8]For we cannot oppose the truth, but must always stand for the truth. [9]We are glad to seem weak if it helps show that you are actually strong. We pray that you will become mature.

13:8
1 Cor 13:6

13:9
1 Cor 2:3; 4:10

[10]I am writing this to you before I come, hoping that I won't need to deal severely with you when I do come. For I want to use the authority the Lord has given me to strengthen you, not to tear you down.

13:10
2 Cor 10:8, 11

13:1 Deut 19:15.   **13:5** Or *in you.*

• **12:20, 21** After reading this catalog of sins, it is hard to believe that these are the people that Paul said possessed great gifts and excelled as leaders (8:7). Paul feared that the practices of wicked Corinth had invaded the congregation. He wrote sternly, hoping that they would straighten out their lives before he arrived. We must live differently from unbelievers, not letting secular society dictate how we are to treat others. Don't let culture influence your behavior.

• **13:2** When Paul arrived the third time in Corinth, he would not be lenient toward unrepentant sinners. His actions could include (1) confronting and publicly denouncing their behavior, (2) exercising church discipline by calling them before the church leaders, or (3) excommunicating them from the church.

13:4 That we "will be alive with him and will have God's power" should be a comfort to all believers. Christians are not just playing church. We are not in this angry ocean of a world in

a rubber raft with a plastic paddle. We are passengers on his Majesty's finest vessel, driven by the indwelling power of the Holy Spirit. We may be tempted to underestimate our ability to accomplish what Christ desires. We forget that Christ is on the bridge, directing the ship safely through the rough seas and finally into its eternal port.

• **13:5** The Corinthians were called to examine and test themselves to see if they really were Christians. Just as we get physical checkups, Paul urges us to give ourselves spiritual checkups. We should look for a growing awareness of Christ's presence and power in our life. Then will we know if we are true Christians or merely impostors. If we're not actively seeking to grow closer to God, we are drawing farther away from him.

13:8, 9 Just as parents want their children to grow into mature adults, so Paul wanted the Corinthians to grow into mature believers. As we share the Good News, our goal should be not merely to see others profess faith or begin attending church but to see them become mature in their faith. Don't set your sights too low.

13:10 The authority Paul had received from the Lord was to strengthen the believers, not to tear them down. Paul gives good advice for our day. Fellow believers are the temple of the Holy Spirit. There is no room in the household of faith for the deprecation of a fellow worker. Before the week is over, write a note of encouragement to several people in your sphere of influence who probably aren't being built up by others in the church. Remind them how much their presence and abilities are needed in your congregation. Express how much you appreciate them.

Paul's Final Greetings

13:11
Rom 15:33
Phil 4:4

[11]Dear brothers and sisters,* I close my letter with these last words: Be joyful. Grow to maturity. Encourage each other. Live in harmony and peace. Then the God of love and peace will be with you.

13:12
Rom 16:16
1 Cor 16:20
1 Pet 5:14

[12]Greet each other with Christian love.* [13]All of God's people here send you their greetings.

13:13
Rom 16:20
Phil 2:1

[14]*May the grace of the Lord Jesus Christ, the love of God, and the fellowship of the Holy Spirit be with you all.

13:11 Greek *Brothers.*   **13:12** Greek *with a sacred kiss.*   **13:14** Some English translations include verse 13 as part of verse 12, and then verse 14 becomes verse 13.

13:11 Paul's closing words—what he wanted the Corinthians to remember about the needs facing their church—are still fitting for the church today. When these qualities are not present, there are problems that must be dealt with. These traits do not come to a church by glossing over problems, conflicts, and difficulties. They are not produced by neglect, denial, withdrawal, or bitterness. They are the by-products of the extremely hard work of solving problems. Just as Paul and the Corinthians had to hammer out difficulties to bring peace, so we must *apply* the principles of God's Word and not just hear them.

13:13 Paul's farewell blessing invokes all three members of the Trinity: Father (God), Son (Lord Jesus Christ), and Holy Spirit. Although the term *Trinity* is not explicitly used in Scripture, verses such as this one show that it was believed and experienced through knowing God's grace, love, and fellowship. See Luke 1:35—the angel Gabriel's announcement of Jesus' birth to Mary; Matthew 3:17—the Father's voice was heard at the baptism of Jesus; and Matthew 28:19—Jesus' commission to the disciples.

13:13 Paul was dealing with an ongoing problem in the Corinthian church. He could have refused to communicate until they cleared up their situation, but he loved them and reached out to them again with the love of Christ. Love, however, means that sometimes we must confront those we care about. Both authority and personal concern are needed in dealing with people who are ruining their lives with sin. But there are several wrong approaches in confronting others, and these can further break relationships rather than heal them. We can be legalistic and blast people away with the laws they should be obeying. We can turn away from them because we don't want to face the situation. We can isolate them by gossiping about their problem and turning others against them as well. Or, like Paul, we can seek to build relationships by taking a better approach—sharing, communicating, and caring. This is a difficult approach that can drain us emotionally, but it is the best way for other people, and it is the only Christlike way to deal with others' sin.

STUDY QUESTIONS

Thirteen lessons for individual or group study

HOW TO USE THIS BIBLE STUDY

It's always exciting to get more than you expect. And that's what you'll find in this Bible study guide—much more than you expect. Our goal was to write thoughtful, practical, dependable, and application-oriented studies of God's word.

This study guide contains the complete text of the selected Bible book. The commentary is accurate, complete, and loaded with unique charts, maps, and profiles of Bible people.

With the Bible text, extensive notes and features, and questions to guide discussion, Life Application Bible Studies have everything you need in one place.

The lessons in this Bible-study guide will work for large classes as well as small-group studies. To get everyone involved in your discussions, encourage participants to answer the questions before each meeting.

Each lesson is divided into five easy-to-lead sections. The section called "Reflect" introduces you and the members of your group to a specific area of life touched by the lesson. "Read" shows which chapters to read and which notes and other features to use. Additional questions help you understand the passage. "Realize" brings into focus the biblical principle to be learned with questions, a special insight, or both. "Respond" helps you make connections with your own situation and personal needs. The questions are designed to help you find areas in your life where you can apply the biblical truths. "Resolve" helps you map out action plans for that day.

Begin and end each lesson with prayer, asking for the Holy Spirit's guidance, direction, and wisdom.

Recommended time allotments for each section of a lesson are as follows:

Segment	60 minutes	90 minutes
Reflect on your life	*5 minutes*	*10 minutes*
Read the passage	*10 minutes*	*15 minutes*
Realize the principle	*15 minutes*	*20 minutes*
Respond to the message	*20 minutes*	*30 minutes*
Resolve to take action	*10 minutes*	*15 minutes*

All five sections work together to help a person learn the lessons, live out the principles, and obey the commands taught in the Bible.

Also, at the end of each lesson, there is a section entitled "More for studying other themes in this section." These questions will help you lead the group in studying other parts of each section not covered in depth by the main lesson.

But don't just listen to God's word. You must do what it says. Otherwise, you are only fooling yourselves. For if you listen to the word and don't obey, it is like glancing at your face in a mirror. You see yourself, walk away, and forget what you look like. But if you look carefully into the perfect law that sets you free, and if you do what it says and don't forget what you heard, then God will bless you for doing it (James 1:22-25).

LESSON 1
HITTING US WHERE WE HURT
2 CORINTHIANS 1:1-11

REFLECT
on your life

1 What does "A chain is only as strong as its weakest link" mean?

_____

_____

_____

_____

2 What is the weakest link in . . .

a team? _____

_____

a business? _____

_____

an individual? _____

_____

READ
the passage

Read the introductory material to 2 Corinthians, 2 Corinthians 1:1-11, and the following notes:

❏ 1:1   ❏ 1:3-5   ❏ 1:5   ❏ 1:6, 7   ❏ 1:8-10

3 Why did Paul write 2 Corinthians?

_____

_____

_____

4 What problems were the Corinthians having?

_____

_____

_____

5 How did Paul address these problems?

_____

_____

_____

6 How did Paul's sufferings benefit his ministry to the Corinthians (1:3-5)?

_____

_____

_____

7 Why were the Corinthians vulnerable to false teachers?

_____

_____

_____

REALIZE
the principle

Second Corinthians is a personal letter from Paul. False teachers had called into question the integrity of his ministry and the very truthfulness of the gospel he was preaching. Paul knew that these false teachers could devastate the new church. Out of his love for Christ and for the believers in Corinth, Paul defended his ministry and the gospel. The Corinthians were weak, their city was immoral, they were being persecuted, and they were young in the faith. They needed to be strengthened. Their example shows us the importance of keeping our focus on Christ and his word. When we lose this focus, we become susceptible to those who would willingly lead us away from Christ. We must remain diligent in our pursuit of Christ.

8 What sufferings were the Corinthians going through that prompted Paul to write about the mercy and comfort of God?

_____

_____

_____

_____

9 How could false teachers exploit the Corinthians' weaknesses?

_____

_____

_____

_____

_____

10 What would make it difficult for Paul to defend himself against the false teachers?

_____

_____

_____

_____

RESPOND
to the message

11 Who are some of today's false teachers?

_____

_____

_____

_____

_____

12 Why are people drawn to false teachers?

_____

_____

_____

_____

13 What weaknesses do false teachers exploit?

_____

_____

_____

_____

_____

14 What can Christians do to strengthen themselves against the lure of false teaching?

_____

_____

_____

_____

_____

_____

15 What weaknesses in your life might make you susceptible to false teaching?

_____

_____

_____

_____

_____

RESOLVE to take action

16 What can you do to strengthen those weak areas?

_____

_____

_____

_____

_____

A What caused Paul to praise God (1:3)? For what can you praise God today?

B What is one reason God comforts us (1:3, 4)? Find other examples in the Bible that point to God's mercy and love as the basis for our expression of mercy and love to others.

C What trouble had Paul endured in Asia (1:8)? What happened as a result of these troubles? What might God be teaching you through the troubles that you are enduring?

MORE for studying other themes in this section

LESSON 2
IN _____ WE TRUST
2 CORINTHIANS 1:12–2:11

1 If someone wanted to borrow $500 from you, what factors would you use to determine whether or not that person was trustworthy?

_____

_____

_____

_____

_____

2 What makes a person trustworthy?

_____

_____

_____

_____

Read 2 Corinthians 1:12–2:11 and the following notes:

❏ 1:15-17   ❏ 1:17-20   ❏ 2:1

3 What caused Paul to change his plans to visit the Corinthians (1:23)?

_____

_____

_____

_____

4 Why did Paul write his painful letter (2:3-4)?

_____

_____

_____

_____

5 What did Paul say to convince the Corinthians that he was trustworthy and committed to them (1:12–2:11)?

_____

_____

_____

_____

6 What should have given the Corinthians confidence in Paul's trustworthiness (1:17-20)?

_____

_____

_____

_____

_____

The Corinthians had some questions for Paul: Why hadn't he visited them as scheduled? Why did he write such a harsh letter to them? Some had begun to wonder if he could even be trusted at all. And if Paul couldn't be trusted to keep his word or to care for them, then maybe the false teachers were right after all—the message brought by Paul might not be absolutely true either. Paul understood why they might be wondering about his reliability. That's why he took such pains to explain his actions to the Corinthians. The evidence was clear: Paul could be trusted. He was a dedicated servant of Christ who always kept his word. His life backed up what he said. He was trustworthy. When others doubt you, what evidence shows that you are trustworthy?

REALIZE
the principle

7 Why was Paul so concerned that the Corinthians understand the reasons for his actions?

_____

_____

_____

_____

8 Why was it important that Paul was trustworthy?

_____

_____

_____

_____

9 How did Paul's integrity come into question?

_____

_____

_____

_____

RESPOND
to the message

10 Why is it important for your behavior to reflect your faith when you talk about God with people?

_____

_____

_____

_____

_____

11 How would you respond to a person who rejects Christianity on the premise that all Christians are hypocrites?

_____

_____

_____

_____

_____

12 What evidence is there that you can be trusted?

_____

_____

_____

_____

13 List one or two areas in your life that you feel do not reflect your faith and that might hinder your witness. Pray about them each day this week. Write down something you would like to do differently by God's grace.

_____

_____

_____

_____

_____

14 What change can you make to give people more confidence in you?

_____

_____

_____

_____

_____

A What does it mean that "all of God's promises have been fulfilled in Christ" (1:20)? Which of God's promises means the most to you?

MORE
for studying
other themes
in this section

B What truths mentioned in 1:21-22 give you security in Christ?

C What is the purpose of church discipline (2:5-11)? What is your role in church discipline?

D What are the schemes of Satan (2:11)? How have you seen them in your life? What steps can you take to see through them?

LESSON 3
THE SURE THING
2 CORINTHIANS 2:12–3:18

REFLECT
on your life

1 What event or happening (besides death and taxes) would you describe as "a sure thing"?

_____

_____

_____

_____

2 What makes you confident of this?

_____

_____

_____

_____

_____

READ
the passage

Read 2 Corinthians 2:12–3:18 and the following notes:

❏ 2:16, 17   ❏ 3:3   ❏ 3:4, 5   ❏ 3:6   ❏ 3:18

3 Why was Paul bold and confident when he talked about Christ (3:4-6, 12)?

_____

_____

_____

_____

4 What can the message of the gospel do (3:6, 9, 18)?

_____

_____

_____

_____

_____

5 What is the basis of our competence to represent God (3:5)?

_____

_____

_____

_____

_____

Paul was bold. That is, he was confident in the gospel and in his ability to deliver it. He believed in his message so strongly that he called it a "life-giving perfume" (2:16). When Paul spoke about Christ, he spoke "with sincerity" (2:17). Such confidence came from God, as a gift, and from the conviction that the gospel could change lives. It's easy to have doubts about ourselves and our ability to communicate. But Christ can give us both the confidence and the competence to deliver his message.

REALIZE
the principle

6 How do people often respond to the gospel message?

_____

_____

_____

_____

7 Why can we be confident about the message of Christ, even if few people believe it?

_____

_____

_____

_____

_____

8 What is the difference between being bold and being obnoxious?

_____

_____

_____

_____

_____

9 How does God want us to live as his ministers?

RESPOND
to the message

_____

_____

_____

_____

10 What doubts sometimes hold you back from representing Christ to the world?

_____

_____

_____

_____

_____

11 How has God given you the competence to represent him?

_____

_____

_____

_____

12 What would make you more confident to represent Christ?

_____

_____

_____

_____

13 To whom do you represent Christ day after day?

_____

_____

_____

_____

_____

RESOLVE
to take action

14 What do you want to remember the next time you doubt your ability to represent Christ to others?

_____

_____

_____

_____

_____

A In what way is the gospel more glorious than the Old Testament law (3:7-11)? What aspects of the law and the gospel are you thankful for?

B What "veils" cover people's minds today (3:14-18)? How can you help lift someone's veil so that person can see Christ clearly and respond to the gospel?

MORE
for studying
other themes
in this section

LESSON 4
DOWNS AND UPS
2 CORINTHIANS 4:1–5:10

1 Finish these sentences:

To a marathon runner, hope is _____

_____

To a football coach, hope is _____

_____

To a salesperson, hope is _____

_____

To a teacher, hope is _____

_____

To a detective, hope is _____

_____

To an investor, hope is _____

_____

To a minimum-wage worker, hope is _____

_____

To a prisoner of war, hope is _____

_____

To a hostage, hope is _____

_____

To a cancer patient, hope is _____

_____

To a Christian, hope is _____

_____

Read 2 Corinthians 4:1–5:10 and the following notes:

❏ 4:8-12   ❏ 4:15-18   ❏ 4:16   ❏ 4:17   ❏ 4:18   ❏ 5:5   ❏ 5:6-8

READ
the passage

2 What was Paul going through that could have caused him to lose hope (4:8-12)?

_____

_____

_____

3 What gave him hope (4:16-18)?

_____

_____

_____

4 How will we be changed when we die (5:1)?

_____

_____

_____

5 How should the final judgment influence how we live now (5:2-10)?

_____

_____

If anyone was aware of his mortality, it was Paul. He suffered a great deal in his travels. But he did not live in despair or stoic detachment. Rather, Paul took hope in the resurrection. He knew that God has a "heavenly body" for each of us. It is easy to become discouraged and lose hope because of our human frailties, weaknesses, and sufferings. When we become too attached to this life, we become susceptible to losing hope. But every Christian will live forever. Every Christian will be raised from the dead. We can take hope in the reality of Christ's promise of a bodily resurrection.

REALIZE
the principle

6 In what ways are we weak and fragile?

_____

_____

_____

_____

7 What can every Christian look forward to?

_____

_____

_____

_____

8 In what do people in our society put their hope?

_____

_____

_____

_____

9 To what escapes do people turn when they feel hopeless?

_____

_____

_____

10 What does the gospel offer to people who feel hopeless?

_____

_____

_____

_____

11 Of which aspect of your mortality are you most aware?

_____

_____

_____

12 What do you look forward to in your future with Christ?

_____

_____

_____

_____

13 What are some ways you can focus your thoughts on "things that cannot be seen" this week (4:18)?

RESOLVE
to take action

_____

_____

_____

_____

_____

14 Whom would you most like to tell about the hope that all in Christ will live forever?

_____

_____

_____

A Why do many people not see the truth of the gospel (4:4)? Who is responsible for changing their mind (4:4-6)? How can you pray for such people in your life?

MORE
for studying
other themes
in this section

B What happens to Christians when they die (5:1-9)? How does this contrast with life on earth? How does this change your perspective on your present problems?

C If we are saved by grace through faith (Ephesians 2:8-9), how is it possible for Christians to be judged "for the good or evil we have done in this earthly body" (2 Corinthians 5:10)? How does the final judgment motivate you to live for Christ?

LESSON 5
SPECIAL DELIVERY
2 CORINTHIANS 5:11– 6:2

REFLECT
on your life

1 What are some ways to deliver a personal message?

_____

_____

_____

_____

_____

_____

2 What's the most unusual way you've ever received a message?

_____

_____

_____

_____

_____

READ
the passage

Read 2 Corinthians 5:11–6:2 and the following notes:

❏ 5:17   ❏ 5:18, 19   ❏ 5:20   ❏ 5:21

3 What message does God want to deliver to the world (5:11–6:2)?

_____

_____

_____

_____

_____

4 What is our part in delivering God's message (5:18-21)?

_____

_____

_____

_____

_____

Paul understood Christ's primary concern: that people be reconciled to God. To be reconciled is to resolve differences between people. To resolve differences between God and people is to introduce them to Christ. Paul's love for Christ motivated him to take the message of Christ to the Corinthians and to others. All Christians are Christ's ambassadors, with a message to deliver. People motivated by the love of Christ look for ways to bring that message to those they care about.

REALIZE
the principle

5 How is reconciliation part of the message God has entrusted to us?

_____

_____

_____

_____

_____

6 Who is God's message for?

_____

_____

_____

_____

_____

7 How can God's message be delivered?

_____

_____

_____

_____

_____

8 What keeps God's message from getting through?

_____

_____

_____

_____

_____

9 What barriers prevent people from accepting the message of reconciliation with Christ?

_____

_____

_____

_____

_____

10 What would make Christians more motivated to tell people about Christ?

_____

_____

_____

_____

11 Whom do you know who personally needs the message of Christ?

_____

_____

_____

12 What can you do to get Christ's message to the people who need it?

_____

_____

_____

_____

_____

_____

13 Write down the names of two unbelievers you know and see regularly. How can you pray for them this week?

RESOLVE
to take action

_____

_____

_____

_____

_____

_____

14 What approach do you prefer for explaining what you believe to your unbelieving friends?

_____

_____

_____

_____

_____

A How is "our fearful responsibility to the Lord" a motivator for ministry (5:11)? What else motivates you to serve God?

B What does it mean to regard someone from a human point of view (5:16)? How should a Christian's perspective be different?

C How did Jesus pay for our sin (5:21)? How can you show your thankfulness?

MORE
for studying
other themes
in this section

LESSON 6
NOT THE DREAM TEAM
2 CORINTHIANS 6:3–7:1

REFLECT
on your life

1 List famous partnerships from . . .

show business _____

_____

politics _____

_____

history _____

_____

the arts _____

_____

sports _____

_____

2 What makes a partnership strong?

_____

_____

_____

_____

3 What makes a partnership weak?

_____

_____

_____

_____

Read 2 Corinthians 6:3–7:1 and the following notes:

❏ 6:14-18   ❏ 6:17

READ
the passage

4 What did Paul mean when he wrote, "Don't team up with those who are unbelievers" (6:14)?

_____

_____

_____

_____

5 Why is such teaming up forbidden (6:14–7:1)?

_____

_____

_____

_____

Corinth was an immoral city, with all the moral ravages one can find in today's cities. In such a sinful setting, God called his people to holiness. What the believers needed to learn was that they could not live for Christ while associating with unbelievers who had such low moral standards. Christ's values and the world's were too different to mix. The same is true today. Christ wants us to be different. In forming ties with unbelievers, we must maintain enough integrity to stay loyal to Christ. Otherwise we will be forced to compromise our beliefs, values, and loyalty.

REALIZE
the principle

6 What causes Christians to form partnerships and alliances with unbelievers?

_____

_____

_____

_____

7 What are the dangers of establishing close ties with unbelievers?

_____

_____

_____

_____

8 What challenges arise from avoiding close ties with unbelievers?

_____

_____

_____

_____

_____

9 In what situations should a Christian not form a partnership with another Christian?

_____

_____

_____

_____

_____

10 What might you say to a Christian high school student who dates an unbeliever?

_____

_____

_____

_____

11 What are two or three examples of Christians teaming up with unbelievers?

_____

_____

_____

12 What should you do if you are already in a partnership with an unbeliever?

_____

_____

_____

_____

_____

13 Regarding the partnerships you are now in, what steps can you take this week to ensure that you don't compromise your Christian commitment?

_____

_____

_____

_____

_____

RESOLVE
to take action

14 What can you do to avoid forming partnerships with unbelievers in the future?

_____

_____

_____

_____

_____

A What hinders people from believing Christians' claims about Christ (6:3)? What can you do to remove such hindrances?

B What experiences did Paul endure in order to avoid discrediting his ministry (6:3-10)? How did Paul's actions help his credibility? What should you be willing to put up with so that people won't find fault with you?

C How can righteousness be used as a weapon (6:7)?

D How do we "cleanse ourselves" (7:1)? What can you do to cleanse yourself?

MORE
for studying
other themes
in this section

LESSON 7
ON THE DEFENSIVE?
2 CORINTHIANS 7:2-16

R **REFLECT**
on your life

1 Imagine you have to confront an employee you like but who is not performing well. How will you begin your conversation?

_____

_____

_____

_____

_____

2 Imagine you are an employee being confronted by a supervisor whom you like. What goes through your mind as your boss starts to speak?

_____

_____

_____

_____

_____

R **READ**
the passage

Read 2 Corinthians 7:2-16, the chart "Principles of Confrontation in 2 Corinthians" (found in chapter 8), and the following notes:

❒ 7:10   ❒ 7:11

3 How did the Corinthians respond to Paul's criticism (7:8-9)?

_____

_____

_____

_____

4 What effect did Paul's confrontation have (7:8-16)?

_____

_____

_____

_____

5 What is the value of "sorrow" (7:10)?

_____

_____

_____

_____

_____

Much of 2 Corinthians is confrontational. In fact, Paul wrote this letter because a face-to-face confrontation would have been too volatile. But the Corinthian believers had received criticism from Paul before, and Paul had only praise for the way they responded. Despite all their problems, the Corinthians responded with "sorrow" when Paul confronted them. Inevitably, Christians find themselves on the receiving end of criticism or confrontation from a person or group. Whether it is justified or not, we need to receive criticism with humility and a genuine desire to learn from it.

6 Why is it difficult to receive criticism?

_____

_____

_____

_____

_____

7 Why do we get defensive when people criticize us, even when we know they're right?

_____

_____

_____

_____

8 Why do people often try to avoid confrontation?

_____

_____

_____

_____

_____

9 Recall a time when you benefited from criticism. What caused the positive outcome?

_____

_____

_____

_____

_____

10 What is the best way to receive criticism, whether it is deserved or not?

_____

_____

_____

_____

_____

11 How have people come to expect you to react to criticism?

_____

_____

_____

_____

12 In what ways do people sometimes react defensively to criticism?

_____

_____

_____

_____

13 What criticism have you already received that you can respond to this week?

RESOLVE
to take action

_____

_____

_____

_____

14 Whom can you thank for their helpful criticism?

_____

_____

_____

_____

A How did Paul feel about the Corinthian believers, despite all their problems (7:2-4)? To whom could you say similar words?

MORE
for studying
other themes
in this section

B How did God use Titus (7:6)? How can God use you?

C How did Titus encourage Paul (7:7)? Whom can you encourage? How can you encourage him/her?

LESSON 8
UNITL IT HURTS!
2 CORINTHIANS 8:1-15

R
REFLECT
on your life

1 Finish this sentence: "I'd give anything to have . . ."

_____

_____

_____

2 What would you have to sacrifice to get what you'd give anything to have?

_____

_____

_____

_____

R
READ
the passage

Read 2 Corinthians 8:1-15 and the following notes:

❏ 8:2-5   ❏ 8:7, 8   ❏ 8:10-15   ❏ 8:12

3 How did the Macedonians give (8:1-5)?

_____

_____

_____

4 What did the Corinthians need to do (8:8-11)?

_____

_____

_____

5 How is Jesus an example of giving (8:9)?

_____

_____

_____

_____

The Macedonian Christians were sacrificial givers. They had little, but they had their priorities straight. They knew that giving was first of all a matter of obedience to God. It was a natural overflow of God's love to want to help others in need. It's easy to think that we'd give "if only we had more" or "if only it didn't cost so much to make ends meet." But God doesn't care about the amount we give. He cares only that the gift is sacrificial. The Macedonian Christians showed us that if we have anything at all, we have something to give to God.

REALIZE
the principle

6 How is giving a "gracious act" (8:7)?

_____

_____

_____

7 What keeps people from giving sacrificially?

_____

_____

_____

8 Why should we give sacrificially?

_____

_____

_____

_____

9 What's the difference between sacrificial giving and irresponsible giving?

_____

_____

_____

_____

RESPOND
to the message

10 Who has been an example of sacrificial giving to you?

_____

_____

_____

_____

11 What have you learned from others about sacrificial giving?

_____

_____

_____

_____

12 What else besides money can you offer to God as a sacrifice?

_____

_____

_____

_____

_____

13 What guidelines should you use to govern your sacrificial giving?

_____

_____

_____

_____

_____

RESOLVE
to take action

14 Look at your budget and spending pattern. How can you change your spending habits to be more reflective of your commitment to Christ?

_____

_____

_____

_____

15 What is the first step in carrying out this change?

_____

_____

_____

_____

_____

A What is the best motive for giving (8:8)? To whom or to what does this motivate you to give?

B How does God take care of those who give to him (8:13-15)? How has God taken care of you?

MORE
for studying
other themes
in this section

LESSON 9
GOD LOVES A CHEERFUL GIVER
2 CORINTHIANS 8:16–9:15

REFLECT
on your life

1 Why do some people think that all the church wants is money?

_____

_____

_____

_____

_____

2 Complete this sentence: People would give more eagerly to the church if . . .

_____

_____

_____

_____

_____

_____

READ
the passage

Read 2 Corinthians 8:16–9:15 and the following notes:

❐ 9:3-5   ❐ 9:6-8   ❐ 9:7   ❐ 9:10   ❐ 9:13

3 How is Christian giving described (8:24; 9:5-6)?

_____

_____

_____

_____

4 What benefits result from giving (9:6, 10-14)?

_____

_____

_____

5 How does God want us to give (9:7)?

_____

_____

_____

_____

6 What does God promise those who give generously (9:6, 8)?

_____

_____

_____

The Corinthians had promised to give money to the church in Jerusalem. In this section of his letter, Paul encouraged them to keep their promise. But even as he did so, he cautioned them to give willingly, "for God loves a person who gives cheerfully" (9:7). It is easy to be cynical about the church's need for money. But God's work needs our support. Whether it is church or missionary work, somebody has to pay the bills. God's people are responsible to do so. And how we give reflects our attitude toward God. That's why God loves giving that comes freely and joyfully from the heart.

REALIZE
the principle

7 What is so important about our attitude in giving?

_____

_____

_____

8 Why does it make sense for us to give cheerfully?

_____

_____

_____

_____

9 What happens when we give cheerfully?

_____

_____

_____

_____

10 When do you find it easy to give cheerfully to God?

_____

_____

_____

_____

11 What motivates you to give?

_____

_____

_____

_____

12 How can you make sure that your giving is not done "reluctantly or in response to pressure" (9:7)?

_____

_____

_____

_____

13 This month, develop a giving plan that will honor God and reflect your heart commitments. If necessary, involve a friend or another Christian who can help you. When can you begin, and who can help you?

_____

_____

_____

_____

A How did Titus and the unnamed workers help Paul (8:16-24)? How can you help God's workers?

B What did Paul do to head off suspicion about the way the gift for the Jerusalem church was delivered (8:18-21)? What precautions can Christians take today to avoid suspicion about their actions?

C What are the advantages and disadvantages of the offering being taken in the worship service at a church? What suggestions do you have for ways collections can be taken and used?

MORE
for studying
other themes
in this section

LESSON 10
"I DON'T MEAN TO BRAG, BUT ..."
2 CORINTHIANS 10:1-18

REFLECT
on your life

1 How do you compare to . . .

Winston Churchill? _____

_____

Adolph Hitler? _____

_____

Johann Sebastian Bach? _____

_____

Jay Leno? _____

_____

Albert Einstein? _____

_____

2 Why do people compare themselves to others?

_____

_____

_____

_____

READ
the passage

Read 2 Corinthians 10:1-18 and the following notes:

❒ 10:12, 13   ❒ 10:17, 18

3 What were the false teachers using as a basis for bragging (10:12)?

_____

_____

_____

4 To what did Paul limit his boasting (10:13-17)?

_____

_____

_____

_____

5 What does it mean to "boast only about the LORD" (10:17)?

_____

_____

_____

6 What difference does it make whether we boast about ourselves or seek God's praise (10:18)?

_____

_____

_____

The false teachers assaulting the Corinthian church were boasters. They compared themselves with others, decided that they were better, and spread the news about their accomplishments. Paul had a different approach. He did not compare himself to others in an effort to demonstrate his superiority or talk down what they had done. He looked at his deeds only in light of what God had given him to do; God would judge them. And if Paul boasted, it would be only about the good he had seen God accomplish through him. In evaluating our accomplishments or our worth, it does not matter how we compare to others. All that matters is whether we have served God as he has called us. It is what God thinks of us—not how we feel or what others think—that counts.

REALIZE
the principle

7 Why do people boast?

_____

_____

_____

8 What do people usually boast about?

_____

_____

_____

9 What is the advantage of seeking God's approval rather than trying to do better than others?

_____

_____

_____

10 How can a Christian "boast only about the LORD" (10:17)?

_____

_____

_____

_____

RESPOND
to the message

11 When are you tempted to compare yourself to others?

_____

_____

_____

_____

12 What usually happens when you compare yourself to others?

_____

_____

_____

13 What actions can help you focus on seeking God's approval rather than on comparing yourself to others?

_____

_____

_____

_____

14 How can you boast about what God has done through you?

_____

_____

_____

_____

15 What can you say (or not say) the next time you do something well?

_____

_____

_____

16 When are you likely to compare your deeds to those of others in the coming week?

_____

_____

_____

_____

_____

RESOLVE
to take action

17 How can you head off the temptation to compare yourself to others?

_____

_____

_____

_____

A How were the false teachers at Corinth trying to discredit Paul (10:1)? What did Paul do about this (10:2-6)? How can you respond to personal attacks?

B What does it mean that "we don't wage war as humans do" (10:3)? What kinds of situations in your life could be seen as spiritual battles? Who are your opponents? How should you fight them?

C Why were the Corinthians being duped by the false teachers (10:7)? How could they have avoided being deceived (10:7-11)? How can you avoid being deceived by false teachers, leaders, or ideas?

MORE
for studying
other themes
in this section

LESSON 11
TRUE OR FALSE?
2 CORINTHIANS 11:1-33

REFLECT
on your life

1 It is often said that imitation is the highest form of flattery. How is this true?

_____

_____

_____

_____

_____

_____

_____

_____

2 When is imitation undesirable or even dangerous?

_____

_____

_____

_____

_____

_____

READ
the passage

Read 2 Corinthians 11:1-33, the chart "Paul's Credentials," and the following notes:

❏ 11:1 ❏ 11:3 ❏ 11:4 ❏ 11:6 ❏ 11:7 ❏ 11:14, 15 ❏ 11:22, 23

❏ 11:23-29

3 Compare Paul with the false apostles (11:1-33):

	Paul	*False Apostles*
Motive	_____	_____
Message	_____	_____
Style of Delivery	_____	_____
Way of Life	_____	_____

4 How do these comparisons show that Paul was the true teacher and the others were not?

_____

_____

_____

5 Why were the Corinthians tempted to believe the false teachers (11:1, 3-4, 18-20)?

_____

_____

_____

6 How can we tell false teachers from true ones (11:4)?

_____

_____

_____

Paul was concerned about the Corinthians. He wanted them to discern wisely so they would not be led astray. They were listening to the lies of the false apostles, and some Corinthian Christians were being led astray from the truth about Christ. Nothing is more important than staying true to the Lord who saved us! It does not pay to be naive. False teachers will often try to lead us away from Christ. That is why we must stay in touch with the word of God.

REALIZE
the principle

7 What are the marks of false teachers? What do they do and say?

_____

_____

_____

_____

8 When is it difficult to identify false teachers?

_____

_____

_____

9 What makes false teachers so attractive?

_____

_____

_____

_____

10 What makes them so dangerous?

_____

_____

_____

RESPOND
to the message

11 How can we tell the difference between true and false spiritual teachers today?

_____

_____

_____

_____

12 Who are some obvious false teachers in our society?

_____

_____

_____

13 Where might we expect to find false teachers?

_____

_____

_____

_____

14 What are some examples of a "different Jesus" that are being preached today?

_____

_____

_____

15 How can we avoid labeling people as false teachers without good reason?

_____

_____

_____

_____

16 What is the most important step you can take right now to discern true teaching from false teaching?

_____

_____

RESOLVE
to take action

_____

_____

_____

_____

A Why was Paul jealous (11:1-3)? For whom do you have a similar concern? How can you share your concern?

B What "shortcoming" of Paul's drew criticism (11:6)? For what shortcomings do people criticize church leaders today? What is a better response than criticism?

C What did Paul do in order to avoid being a burden to the Corinthians (11:7-9)? What can you do to avoid being a burden to those you serve?

D Why did Paul defend himself (11:10-12)? What was at stake? What is worth defending to you?

E What did Paul do that he called foolish (11:16-29)? When might you be driven to "foolishness" in order to defend the gospel?

MORE
for studying
other themes
in this section

LESSON 12
A THORNY SITUATION
2 CORINTHIANS 12:1-10

REFLECT
on your life

1 What are some limitations of . . .

being young? _____

_____

having children? _____

_____

being single? _____

_____

being retired? _____

_____

your current financial situation? _____

_____

2 What limitation would you get rid of if you could?

_____

_____

_____

READ
the passage

Read 2 Corinthians 12:1-10 and the following notes:

❒ 12:7, 8   ❒ 12:9   ❒ 12:10

3 Why did Paul receive a "thorn in [the] flesh" (12:7)?

_____

_____

_____

4 Where did the thorn come from (12:7)?

_____

_____

_____

5 What did God want Paul to learn from this weakness (12:9)?

_____

_____

_____

6 How did Paul's attitude about his weakness change (12:8-10)?

_____

_____

_____

Life wasn't any easier for the apostle Paul than it is for us. Rather than being excused from life's problems for his faith, Paul was called by Christ to live with a limitation that frustrated him. Over time, this "messenger from Satan" taught Paul to depend on God, making Paul even more useful to God than without it. He earnestly asked God to remove his weakness, yet God said no. Eventually Paul learned to welcome this "thorn" as a way for God to demonstrate his power through him. Who can't identify with Paul's plight? The weaknesses, hardships, insults, persecutions, and difficulties we live with are opportunities to rely on God and see him work in spite of our limitations.

REALIZE
the principle

7 List some of the feelings and thoughts that Paul might have had as he asked God to remove his "thorn."

_____

_____

_____

_____

8 Why should a person welcome a frustrating experience or weakness?

_____

_____

_____

_____

9 How can a person welcome frustrating experiences or weaknesses?

_____

_____

_____

_____

10 How does grace help a person with a frustrating problem?

_____

_____

_____

_____

RESPOND
to the message

11 What are some weaknesses or hardships that frustrate you?

_____

_____

_____

_____

_____

12 How can God use these difficulties?

_____

_____

_____

_____

_____

13 In what practical ways can you rely on God when you are limited by weaknesses and hardships?

_____

_____

_____

_____

_____

14 How might you counsel someone who is frustrated by a weakness or difficulty?

_____

_____

_____

_____

15 How can you pray about your frustrating situations this week?

_____

_____

_____

_____

_____

RESOLVE
to take action

16 What can you do the next time you face a frustrating weakness or difficulty?

_____

_____

_____

_____

_____

A What unique experience did Paul have (12:2-4)? What unique experience has drawn you closer to God?

B Why did Paul refrain from boasting about his walk with God (12:6)? What should you refrain from boasting about?

MORE
for studying
other themes
in this section

LESSON 13
LOOK WHO'S BOSS
2 CORINTHIANS 12:11–13:14

REFLECT
on your life

1 What might authority be to a . . .

dictator? _____

_____

missionary? _____

_____

billionaire? _____

_____

coach? _____

_____

congressperson? _____

_____

construction foreman? _____

_____

2 All of the people above have authority. What are the differences in how they use it?

_____

_____

_____

_____

READ
the passage

Read 2 Corinthians 12:11–13:13 and the following notes:

❏ 12:11-15   ❏ 12:20, 21   ❏ 13:2   ❏ 13:5

3 Why should the Corinthians have accepted Paul's authority (12:11-13)?

_____

_____

_____

4 How did Paul use his authority (12:19)?

_____

_____

_____

_____

5 What did Paul fear would happen when he visited the Corinthians a third time (12:20-21)?

_____

_____

_____

_____

6 How did Paul plan to use his authority when he visited again (13:1-3, 10)?

_____

_____

_____

Throughout 2 Corinthians Paul stressed that he had legitimate authority, given by Jesus Christ himself. Yet Paul did not use his authority for his own gain. He did not use it to increase his stature, reputation, or financial position. Rather, he used it to strengthen the Christians at Corinth. Whether a volunteer coach or a paid employee, a person having authority has a special responsibility—to be a source of blessing to those under him/her. Authority that serves and builds up others is the kind that has God's approval.

REALIZE
the principle

7 How can authority be used to build people up?

_____

_____

_____

_____

8 When is it good for those with authority to be strict with those under them?

_____

_____

_____

_____

9 What is the difference between legitimate and illegitimate uses of authority?

_____

_____

_____

_____

_____

10 Over whom are you in authority right now?

RESPOND
to the message

_____

_____

_____

_____

11 How do you think others view your use of authority? Do they see you building people up or tearing people down?

_____

_____

_____

_____

12 What can you do to bring your authority under the guidance and control of God and to use it to build up others?

_____

_____

_____

_____

_____

13 Name at least one area of your life where you have some authority over another person. How can you use that authority this week to build up that person?

R
RESOLVE
to take action

_____

_____

_____

_____

_____

_____

14 For what person in authority can you pray this week?

_____

_____

_____

_____

A How can you know if your "faith is genuine" (13:5)? What steps can you take to grow closer to God?

MORE
for studying
other themes
in this section

B What does it mean for Christians to "greet each other with Christian love" (13:12)? How might you reflect your commitment to Christ in the way you greet others?

C How did Paul close this letter of confrontation (13:14)? How can you show similar concern for the ones you love?

Take Your Bible Study
to the Next Level

The **Life Application Study Bible** helps you apply truths in God's Word to everyday life. It's packed with nearly 10,000 notes and features that make it today's #1–selling study Bible.

Life Application Notes: Thousands of Life Application notes help explain God's Word and challenge you to apply the truth of Scripture to your life.

Personality Profiles: You can benefit from the life experiences of over a hundred Bible figures.

Book Introductions: These provide vital statistics, an overview, and a timeline to help you quickly understand the message of each book.

Maps: Over 200 maps next to the Bible text highlight important Bible places and events.

Christian Worker's Resource: Enhance your ministry effectiveness with this practical supplement.

Charts: Over 260 charts help explain difficult concepts and relationships.

Harmony of the Gospels: Using a unique numbering system, the events from all four Gospels are harmonized into one chronological account.

Daily Reading Plan: This reading plan is your guide to reading through the entire Bible in one unforgettable year.

Topical Index: A master index provides instant access to Bible passages and features that address the topics on your mind.

Dictionary/Concordance: With entries for many of the important words in the Bible, this is an excellent starting place for studying the Bible text.

Available in the New Living Translation, New International Version, King James Version, and New King James Version. Take an interactive tour of the *Life Application Study Bible* at
www.NewLivingTranslation.com/LASB

CP0271